Companion Guide for Speech

Companion Guide for Speech & Debate Coaches

Molly K. Beck

Shawn F. Briscoe

Amy J. Johnson

Edited by Shawn F. Briscoe

MY DEBATE RESOURCES

My Debate Resources
www.mydebateresource.com

Cover design by www.ebooklaunch.com

Cover illustrations: photographs by Shawn F. Briscoe (author/editor) (*clockwise from top: 1, 2, 4, and 5*) and by Shane Ohms (3); pictured clockwise from top (*Mark H., Austin H., Terek R. [left], Skyler H. [right], Sarah C., Taylor P. [right], Jamal B. [left]*); all images used with permission.

Names: Briscoe, Shawn F., author / editor
        Beck, Molly K., author
        Johnson, Amy J., author
Title: Companion Guide for Speech & Debate Coaches / Shawn F. Briscoe
Description: My Debate Resources [2017]
Identifiers: ISBN 978-0-9978684-2-5 (paperback);
  ISBN978-0-9978684-3-2 (e-book)

This book is for all the coaches, judges, and volunteers that give their time, energy, and expertise to students so that they may better understand the world and gain the tools to improve themselves and the world around them.

Mom & Dad – Thank you for raising me to follow my dreams and for believing in me. Mom, Dad, Lexi, & Carly – Thank you for the endless encouragement, support, and love. In memory of Toni Schaper and Robert Beck who are so much of who I am. ~Molly

Becky, Ben, & Hannah – Thank you for being the best family a guy could have! Mom – Thanks for always lending an ear. ~Shawn

Ben for supporting me through all the practices and performances, and to my parents for allowing the love of theatre to develop. ~Amy

Acknowledgements

This book is a compilation of ideas we developed over our coaching careers. We tried to limit those ideas to only those things we developed ourselves. As with any teaching endeavor and years of experience, we recognize it is inevitable that we have picked up and shared ideas through conversations, competitions, and other interactions. Nevertheless, we did our best to ensure we were sharing our own ideas and not those of others. There are a handful of exceptions. For example, we got the idea for writing notes to teachers from the students in Alaska who have done that for years. Unfortunately, we have no way of crediting those types of best practices to a specific individual. Several of the recruiting tips came from the creative mind of Becky — Shawn's wife. Because of that creative bleeding, we would be remiss if we did not thank our mentors, peers, and students with whom we have had the honor of working with over the years: Nevada High School and the Carver Truman district (especially Tim Gore, Ed Grooms, Deborah Workman, & Dennis Pendrak); Fort Walton Beach High School (especially Ann Hicks & Sean Luechtefeld); Houghton High School (especially John Griebel); Missouri State University Theatre Department (especially Jamie Deckard, CJ Maples, Melissa Harper, Tim Haynes, & Adam Murphy); U.S. Air Force Academy (especially David Jesurun, Ryan Davis, & Marshall McMullen); University of Alaska Anchorage (especially Steve Johnson, Janet Steinhauser, Paul Ongtooguk, Becky James, & Roger Miller); Parkway School District (especially Gayle Elzinga, Jennifer Forrest-James, Michael Hachmeister, & Nicole Voss); Robert Service High School (especially Deborah Benson, Chad Sant, & JP Tarbath); South Anchorage High School (especially Katy Bishoff & Maria Skala); the staff and faculty of Homer High School, the entire Alaska Drama, Debate & Forensics community, Springfield (MO) coaching community (especially Bill Jordan & Teresa Sparkman), and the Eastern Missouri speech & debate community (especially Cara Borgsmiller, Justin Seiwell, & Robyn Haug).

Table of Contents

Preface: A Philosophy of Coaching

By Shawn F. Briscoe

After serving ten years in the United States Air Force, I decided to transition from a career as a military officer to one as a high school teacher and debate coach. In part, I made this change because I believed my talents could be put to more effective use serving this society in an educational setting. I also made this move because I believe schools play an integral role in developing the human mind, thereby helping individuals reach their fullest potential and society advance alongside them. My role as an educator has been shaped, significantly, by some of the great philosophers such as Plato, Aristotle, and John Stuart Mill; several feminist authors; as well as the promises contained in the Declaration of Independence and the Constitution of the United States.

Before delving into my approach to coaching, I must clarify a few assumptions that frame how I coach. First and foremost, as a debate coach, my central role is that of an educator. In this capacity, I help grow students into responsible, productive, and engaged citizens. Second, I have a responsibility to care for young people. Parents and guardians entrust me to keep their children safe, to provide for their well-being, and so forth. These are the driving forces behind my philosophy of coaching. I do not, however, place an emphasis on competitive achievements. My purpose is not to receive accolades, accumulate trophies, or collect championships. Rather, I serve students through the mission of our educational system.

Thus, I should explain my view of *what school is all about*. Getting an education is about discovering the truth. By *truth*, I mean how the world works, why it works the way it does, how it ought to be, and so forth. Since I also believe the journey is never complete, the discovery of truth is a life-long process. Thus, one of the critical aspects of getting an education is the notion of learning how to learn. For this quest to succeed, we must all gain a broad-based or liberal education. At its core, this involves the typical disciplines of math, science, English, and social studies. However, to truly understand the world around us, we must also study the philosophies and the arts. At the same time, we gain valuable insight by taking part in a variety of extracurricular activities such as social clubs, competitive teams, and sports. All these disciplines offer unique insight into the world, help develop well-rounded individuals, and teach us how to interact with others in responsible and effective ways.

Similarly, to gain complete perspective, we must be surrounded by people from different backgrounds and exposed to multiple viewpoints. As such, a critical function of schools is to bring together people from various walks of life and offer a variety of viewpoints on the subjects they cover. Ultimately, this quest for understanding develops informed citizens and enables us to find solutions to society's problems. For example, professor of political science and education, Walter Parker explains that "engaged citizens do not materialize out of thin air. They do not naturally grasp such knotty principles as tolerance, impartial justice, the separation of church and state, the needs for limits on majority power, or the difference between liberty and license" (2006, 49). To truly grasp these principals, students must be exposed to the philosophical roots and history surrounding these ideas. They must read literature written by people on all sides of the issues. They must engage one another on each of these topics to truly understand their relevance, their shortcomings, and their promise for the future.

Furthermore, this quest for knowledge and understanding is empowering for the individual. One group of San Francisco State University professors of education concluded that "liberatory acts are deeply rooted in critical dialogue, critical reflection, and praxis" (Arce, Luna, Borjian, & Conrad, 2005, 69). Intellectually, an education is necessary for an individual to reach his or her fullest potential. Individually, an education can empower that individual to overcome barriers that prevent the realization of that goal. Collectively, an education can also help individuals--in both the minority and majority--destroy the barriers that prevent the realization of equality in our society. This notion is not unique to the area of social justice; it can also be applied to any number of areas ranging from economics to international politics.

As such, it should be our goal as educators to ensure that everyone is afforded the opportunity for a critical and broad education. Philosophically it makes sense because everyone has worth and is entitled to the benefits of an education. Practically it makes sense because everyone brings unique contributions to society and can ultimately help it evolve. These beliefs about individuals, our society, and education, have a significant influence on my approach to coaching.

First, I believe that everyone has the innate ability to learn and should be welcomed in an academic environment. Plato expressed this idea succinctly over two thousand years ago when he explained that "the capacity to learn… [is] present in every person" (1992, 162). Everyone is capable of learning, and everyone deserves an equal and equitable opportunity to take part in the learning process. Furthermore, accepting the idea that some are incapable of learning promotes a system that gives up on those individuals, leads to self-fulfilling prophecies, and denies individuals the opportunity of rising above their current state of being. Thus, any system that determines a group of individuals is beyond learning is a flawed one.

I personally saw this truism play out on several occasions during my first year of teaching. I saw it in my students when other teachers told me that my *Level 1* readers could not handle the readings or the concepts that I was having them study. Nevertheless, they managed to struggle through scholarly journal articles on globalization and international politics and develop their own opinions and arguments on the topics. I saw it when a substitute for those same students told them he was ditching my lesson plan because I was filling their heads with "liberal and fascist ideas." They, in turn, informed him that unlike with his narrow view, I gave them multiple sides of the issue so they could develop their own stance. I saw it in one of my seniors who used his understanding of readings from social ecologists, professors of intercultural communication, and John Stuart Mill to develop his own criticism of Foucault's thoughts on power, knowledge, and discourse. All of these situations demonstrated the ability of students to think and achieve beyond what was considered normal and appropriate for them. Thus, they reinforced my belief that everyone is capable of learning and encouraged me to challenge students in the future.

Second, my role as a coach is to guide the students in their learning endeavors. As Plato explained in *The Republic*, education "is not the art of putting the capacity of sight into the soul; the soul possesses that already but it is not turned the right way or looking where it should. This is what education has to deal with" (1992, 162). In other words, students are not empty jars to be filled with knowledge by the teacher. I am not there simply to impart knowledge. My role is to serve as a guide, helping them explore various topics and develop their own understanding of them. In part, this requires them to be active in the process of learning. However, I must find ways to help motivate them to study the topics. Furthermore, I should challenge their assumptions, forcing them to identify flaws in their thinking, reconsider their points of view, and/or have a deeper understanding of and commitment to their beliefs. In sum, education is not about me giving students the *truth*. Rather, it is about them figuring out the answers for themselves.

Finally, as I alluded to above, I believe it is important to expose students to multiple points of view while guarding against letting them know my personal stance on controversial issues. In other words, the classroom should be organized so that it fosters in-depth, multi-directional discussions among the students and teacher. During these discussions, students should feel free to express doubt and point to what they see as shortcomings in the arguments and perspectives presented to them. At the same time, it is my responsibility to help them build frameworks for understanding those issues. In addition, I should help them develop the tools they need to develop well-thought out arguments that support their views. Thankfully, speech and debate inherently explores those issues and develops these frameworks. In this way, if students are given this freedom to think issues through, they are much more likely to truly grasp the theories and their implications for the world around them. Furthermore, approaching school from this direction empowers students to develop their own novel approaches to societal problems. If they are given the freedom to truly learn the subject matter, they are infinitely more likely to use that knowledge in everyday life.

In short, I believe education is a continual search for the truth. No one has all the answers. However, collectively we can study the past and the present to develop a clearer understanding of reality. As students progress along this journey, they are empowered to become more than they used to be. For me to facilitate their progress, I must remember that everyone is capable of learning, expose students to myriad viewpoints, and serve as a guide in helping them understand the world around them.

References

Arce, J., Luna, D., Borjian, A., & Conrad, M. (2005). No Child Left Behind: Who wins? Who loses. *Social Justice: A Journal of Crime, Conflict & World Order*, 32(3), 56-71.

Parker, W. C. (2006). Teaching against idiocy. In F. Schultz (Ed.), *Annual editions: Education 06/07* (pp. 47-52). Dubuque, IA: McGraw-Hill. Reprinted from *Phi Delta Kappan*, 344-351, January 2005)

Plato. (1992). *The republic* (G. M. A. Grube, Trans.). In M. L. Morgan (Ed.), *Classics of moral and political theory* (pp. 31-231). Indianapolis, IN: Hackett Publishing Company. Reprinted from *Plato's republic*, 1974, Indianapolis, IN: Hackett Publishing Company.

Team Management

Recruiting

Recruiting Tip

Having trouble recruiting students? Often, students and teachers just don't know our teams exist, nor do they necessarily know who they should be directing to us.

Stand up at the next faculty meeting and tell everyone about the activity and your squad. Include highlights from last year. Let them know that debate isn't just for "honors kids." The students who need it the most are the ones who might be struggling academically. Let them know that debate isn't just for vocal extroverts. The quiet kids and introverts are often the best debaters, speakers, and interpers. Then, ask everyone there to give you two names of students before they leave. Better yet, bring scrap sheets of paper for them to write on. Then, get a personal invitation to every name you collect… be sure to tell the students they were recommended by one of their teachers. The more personalized the message, the more likely they are to show up to your team's next meeting.

In addition to talking to your peers, circulate flyers or letters around the school. Some examples of documents I share with students and staff include "Dispensing with the Myths of Speech & Debate," letters to faculty about our program, and posters tailored to our team.

Ladue Horton Watkins
High School
Talking Rams

Dear Tyanna Baker,

Greetings! We would like to take this opportunity to welcome you back for another year at Ladue Horton Watkins High School! We hope this year will be exciting and challenging for you. We know there are many opportunities for involvement at the high school, and we sincerely hope you will choose to join the Talking Rams, the speech and debate team.

The speech and debate team is recognized at the local, state, and national level as being a premier and high achieving team. In the 2011-2012 school year the team members won trophies at every single tournament in both speech and debate events. The Talking Ram's most notable achievements in the past year include:

- First place in the Greater Saint Louis Speech Association's tournament
- One student being invited to attend two national circuit tournaments – the student won recognition at both tournaments
- Three students earning spots at the MSHSAA State Speech and Debate tournament – one student triple-qualified
- Winning the National Speech & Debate Association (NSDA) District Tournament and sending eight students to the NSDA National Championship Tournament
- Quarterfinalist in debate at the MSHSAA State Tournament
- 4-time qualifier to the NSDA National Championship Tournament
- 10th place in Extemporaneous Speaking at the National Catholic Forensic League Grand National Tournament
- Quarterfinalist in Extemporaneous Speaking at the NSDA National Championship Tournament
- 16th place in Policy Debate at the NSDA National Championship Tournament
- Speech and Debate Student of the Year for the entire Saint Louis area

Your name was given to us because someone believes you will excel in speech and debate. We would like you to come to our first meeting, Monday, 20 August 2012 in room 251 after school. You'll have an opportunity to learn about the team and the upcoming year as well as meet captains and other students. Plan to stay after school on Tuesday and Wednesday to learn about the different competition events. Thursday will be the first debate practice! Please bring a friend to the meeting as well! See Miss Beck in room 251 or the English Office if you have questions. You may also e-mail her at mbeck@ladueschools.net. We hope to see you on Monday!

Go Rams!
Miss Beck   Aramis Rickey
Head Coach   Team President

Dispensing with the Myths of Speech & Debate

Myth #1: Forensics is about examining dead bodies
Fact: Forensics is the study of rhetoric, and includes elements of speech, debate, and the interpretation of literature (similar to acting).

Myth #2: We are only looking for honors-type students.
Fact: Many of the most successful forensics students are not at the top of their class. Furthermore, those not at the top have the most to gain from participating in the activity.

Myth #3: Debaters are out-spoken, extroverts.
Fact: Some of the best debaters are much more reserved. Many are shy, introverts.

Myth #4: Competitive forensics involves speaking in front of large audiences.
Fact: Typically, a competitor is speaking in front of a judge, a timekeeper, and his or her opponent(s). We rarely have large audiences until the championship round.

Myth #5: Competitive drama students come from a background in theater.
Fact: While theater and interpretation (aka-drama) often overlap, there are major differences. In theater, an actor becomes a part. In competitive drama, an actor needs to be able to quickly transform from one believable character to another in an effort to bring meaning to a story.

Myth #6: Participants spend their day sitting in a room, while listening to others talk.
Fact: Speech and Debate is *intellectual combat*, making friends, and travelling to interesting places like Boston, Las Vegas, Ft. Lauderdale, and Washington D.C.

Sample Letter to Faculty

August 17, 2011

The South Anchorage Drama, Debate, & Forensics team is ready to kick off the season. Please take a moment to view the attached documents and learn a little about our team.

We would also appreciate it if you would share this information with your classes. If you have any students you think would be particularly suited to public speaking, debating both sides of an issue (not just one side), or can take on multiple personas within a single acting piece, please encourage them to check us out.

I would also like to dispel a few preconceived notions that many people have:

Myth #1: Forensics programs are only looking for honors-type students.
> Fact: Many of the most successful forensics students are not at the top of their class. Those not at the top have the most to gain from participating in the activity.

Myth #2: Debaters are out-spoken, extroverts.
> Fact: Some of the best debaters are much more reserved. I, for one, was the introverted, quiet kid in school who only spoke in class when the teacher called on me.

Myth #3: Competitive forensics involves speaking in front of large audiences.
> Fact: Most often, a competitor is speaking in front of a judge, a timekeeper, and his or her opponent(s). We rarely have large audiences until the championship round.

Myth #4: Competitive drama students come from a background in theater.
> Fact: While theater and interpretation can often overlap, there are major differences. In interp, students take on multiple personas to illuminate meaning within a story.

We will have a series of organizational meetings from 2:10-3:45 on Mondays and Wednesdays starting August 17th, in G204. Beginning August 31st, our practices start at those same times. Activities fees will be due on September 12th; however, students in other activities may join our squad later in the year. We encourage all interested students to drop by our organizational meetings right away to learn about what we do. We are also holding an informational meeting during *lunch* on *Tuesday, August 23rd (G204)*.

Thanks for spreading the word about our program. If you have any questions about us, don't hesitate to contact me (**briscoe_shawn@asdk12.org**).

Sincerely,

Shawn Briscoe
Director DDF & Debate Coach

Create a Flyer for Your Team

South Anchorage HS Forensics Team
aka - Drama, Debate & Forensics

Forensics is a team and individual sport that includes debate, public speaking, and literary/dramatic performance. The activity teaches students to work collaboratively; build confidence; improve critical thinking, research, and organizational skills; and develop presentation techniques.

Competing with the team can earn an individual membership in the National Speech & Debate Association (NSDA) - an academic honor society recognized by colleges throughout the nation. Since 2004, the Wolverines have had 26 individual state champions and 75 national championship tournament qualifiers. In addition, the entire squad won the 2009 (photo at right), 2011, 2012, & 2013 Debate State Championship, the 2011 & 2012 Forensics Championship, and the 2011 & 2012 overall DDF Championship. Furthermore, the NSDA ranked the squad the top program in Alaska every year from 2009-2012, and ranked it in the top 10% of programs in the nation for 2011 & 2012.

SAT/ACT: Score Well on Tests
A report by Yale University reports that participation in speech and debate activities increases standardized test scores *more than taking expensive test prep courses.*

Top College Admissions
A 1999 report in the *Wall Street Journal* cited forensics as **the top extra-curricular activity college admissions counselors look for,** especially where enrollment is competitive, such as Ivy League schools.

Who we are and what we do:

✓ Like Track & Field, forensics involves strategy and coaching and is comprised of multiple events, requiring different skills.
✓ Emphasizes two of the most overlooked areas of literacy; speaking and listening. Students are exposed to critical thinking situations and an elevated vocabulary, which they practice.
✓ It is cross-curricular, drawing heavily upon social sciences. Requires students to critically engage in analysis of issues, problems and characterizations. They are exposed to diverse perspectives of other students through communication and the "Marketplace of Ideas" to become active members of our democratic society.
✓ "[H]as the power to inspire students to learn and help them grasp the concepts we aim to instill." - **Education Next, Winter '09**

Forensics at South Anchorage HS:
We participate in local and national competitions, making great friends. We've been to: Harvard University; University of Nevada-Las Vegas; Birmingham, AL; Dallas, TX; Kansas City, MO; Omaha, NE; Washington, DC; Homer & Sitka, AK.
Contact us *at:* shawn.briscoe@uaa.alaska.edu

Local tournaments are held on Fridays and Saturdays. The competitive season runs from October through February. Competitors may earn a spot at State in March and one of two national championship tournaments during the summer.

"Forensics... should be a meaningful part of every school's curriculum... [T]he course of study, alongside cocurricular competition, promotes civic education and enhances the standard curriculum by helping students explore myriad topics from multiple angles and find the truth in each, fostering civic participation, advocating civic engagement, promoting authentic discussions on issues of real importance, and emphasizing the principles that are essential to a liberal democracy."
- Principal Leadership, May '09

IMPROVE YOUR SPEAKING AND MAKE GREAT FRIENDS

LADUE SPEECH
& DEBATE TEAM

TALKING
RAMS

Mondays-Thursdays | After
School-Around 4pm
Rm. 227, Ms. Becks Room

ewu86@ladueschools.net

ldyson44@ladueschools.net

HTTP://TALKINGRAMS.WEEBLY.COM/

Sample Letter to Parents of Prospective Students

Dear Parents and Guardians

I am the head coach for South Anchorage High School's Drama, Debate, & Forensics program. A new season is upon us, and I eagerly anticipate a fun-filled and successful year. What we do will build substantially upon what our students learn in the general education curriculum. At times, this means the student will be required to perform additional work… as with any extracurricular, competitive team. I firmly believe that forensics provides a solid foundation upon which all other academic and professional goals can be built. Throughout the season we will compete regularly, have the opportunity to travel the country, build the bonds of a team, and make friends with people who come from different walks of life than our own. Meanwhile, we will learn about current events, philosophy, critical thinking skills, argumentation techniques, persuasive speaking skills, how to analyze literature, and so forth. Then, we will have the opportunity to practice what we learned in a unique competitive environment.

Let me begin by letting you know a few things about me. Before moving into the teaching profession, I spent 6 years on active duty in the U.S. Air Force. During this time, I was surrounded by amazing people and had some very unique experiences. I also learned a lot about myself and people, in general. A great deal of my responsibilities involved counseling young people, mentoring new supervisors, and leading a diverse group of folks. I learned that the best way to lead and motivate people was to work with them, rather than dictate policies they must obey. I found that if individuals had an opportunity to express themselves and take part in the process — to the extent possible — they were much more likely to take ownership in the process and devote themselves to accomplishing their jobs.

What does this have to do with me teaching/coaching your child? After 6 years, I wanted to pay back the wonderful mentors and teachers that I had in high school by becoming a teacher myself. Specifically, I chose to give back by becoming a speech & debate coach because I believed my teachers/coaches in this discipline had a profound impact on my later successes. From an academic standpoint, I look forward to exploring the discipline of forensics alongside your student. Only by actively looking at the "big questions" together can they truly come to grasp the lessons the world has to teach *us*.

While I am the coach and we have an exceptional coaching staff, I want your sons and daughters to be actively involved in creating something meaningful out of this activity. Thus, we are here to serve as leaders, mentors, and guides. Along our journey, we will all work side-by-side to learn, have fun, and reap the rewards of success.

Throughout the year, we will have the opportunity to compete in 6-10 tournaments. The local tournaments and state are largely paid for by the district. However, if your child wants to attend our trip out of state or qualifies for the national championships, we will need to engage in some fundraising.

I sincerely look forward to the upcoming year. If you have any questions or would like to meet with me, please contact me by phone at (907) 555-6200 or e-mail at **briscoe_shawn@asdk12.org**.

Sincerely,
SHAWN F. BRISCOE
Head DDF Coach

Recruiting Drive

Still looking for ways to grow your squad? Try having a targeted recruiting drive. Advertise the upcoming "information meeting" throughout the school... posters, morning announcements, flyers in teachers' mailboxes. Have all returning members invite (aka – drag) someone from one of their classes to the meeting. For small teams, require returning members to bring two people. Begin the meeting by giving potential recruits an idea of what forensics (speech & debate) is, what the season looks like, who they compete against, some of the benefits of participating, etc. Most importantly, have returning members share what they love about the activity. Try to collect contact information (e-mail addresses for the students and their parents/guardians) before they leave. Then, follow up with them before the next practice.

Pro Tip: Talk to your principal or athletic director about providing pizza. Even with limited budgets, many ADs/principals will see this as a drop in the bucket. You may need to grease the wheels by explaining the benefits of the program to the school, as well.

Introduction to Forensics

During the first practice with prospective team members, you will want to spend time getting to know one another, sharing why returning members are on the team, familiarizing recruits with the events, highlighting the season calendar, and so forth. It is also helpful to give them a glimpse of what the activity looks like. At some point during the meeting, take a break to have returning members demonstrate some of the events.

Step 1: Have a returning extemper draw three questions, and send him or her into the hall to prep. (*Feel free to share the three questions with your student well in advance, but go through the motions so new students can see what the process looks like in competition.*)

Step 2: Have a returning interper perform his or her piece from last year.

Step 3: Have two students (or two teams of two) demonstrate a mock debate. Use typical strategies, but do not use cards (aka – quoted evidence). Suggested format: 1AC – CX – 1NC – CX – 1AR – 1NR. (*All speeches are 4 minutes; CX is 2 minutes; 1 or 2 minutes of prep time before each speech.*) The topic should be easily accessible. Examples – Resolved: School districts should grant academic credit for participation on debate teams. Resolved: School districts should use corporal punishment. Resolved: States should require two semesters of participation in competitive extracurricular activities for high school graduation. Resolved: Districts should require school uniforms in public schools. (*I once had three students debate the topic Resolved: Participation in debate should be a high school graduation requirement. I had my top Lincoln Douglas debater present a typical LD case on one side, while my top policy debate team responded with typical policy analysis such as harms mitigators, case turns, and a disadvantage.*)

Step 4: Call the extemper back into the room to present his or her speech.

Step 5: At this meeting or the next, collect contact information for your students and their parents/guardians. Throughout the season, you will need to communicate with them about future events. While attending tournaments, you will need the ability to communicate with both parents and students, especially if your team travels outside the local area.

Team Membership Form

Student Name: _____

Nickname (If Applicable): _____

Grade Level for 2016-2017: _____

Level of Competition (Circle One):   NOVICE   JUNIOR VARSITY   VARSITY

Student Cell Phone Number: _____

Parent/Guardian Name(s): _____

Parent/Guardian Evening/Weekend Phone Number: _____

Parent/Guardian Evening/Weekend Phone Number: _____

Parent/Guardian E-mail Address: _____

Parent/Guardian E-mail Address: _____

Primary Address:

_____

_____

Secondary Address (if applicable):

_____

_____

Community Building

One of the most important things you can do at the start of the season is build a sense of community. Look for activities that get students working together and getting to know each other. If you are like Shawn, your focus for the year will be on education and having fun… express that early. Let students know your expectations.

During your first practice after recruiting new members, go around the room and have students introduce themselves. Give them the following questions:

Returning Students: Name? How many years have you been on the team? Why did you join the team? What do you love most about the activity?

New Students: Name? Why do you want to join the team? What do you hope to get from being on the team?

Once introductions are out of the way, play games to get them excited about the team and getting to know one another. Some examples include, Spontaneous Debates, Moods, Charades, Cranium, SPAR CARDS, and Spark: the ultimate improv game. All game selections should be fun, but also draw out some of the skills developed in speech & debate.

Planning for the Season

Team Handbook

Coaches should always provide clear expectations to students *and* parents. I highly recommend creating a team handbook that can be distributed during the first few practices of the year. This handbook should include team rules, practice expectations, a tournament schedule, and so forth. I have included a slightly modified handbook that I used when I coached at South Anchorage High School that can serve as an example of something you might create for your team. Different coaches and teams will need different levels of details in their handbooks. Some may be very short (1-2 pages) others may be quite lengthy (15-20 pages). The amount of detail largely depends on your comfort level as a coach and the personality of your team.

DDF Team Handbook
South Anchorage High School
2011-12 School Year

This handbook covers the things you need to know to have a happy, productive Drama, Debate, & Forensics (DDF) season. Please read this and show it to your parents. You must also turn in a signed contract. We are looking forward to working with you this year.

Joining the Team

You may attend practices once you have turned in your activity fee and form to the Activities Office. Check with the Activities Office if you need an activity fee waiver. You also need to turn in a team contract to me, signed by you and your parent/guardian. At that point, you are an official member of the team.

Contact Information

Please fill out a contact information sheet at your first practice. That way, we'll have information on how to contact you and your parents. The coaches' contact information is provided for your benefit.

<u>Mr Shawn Briscoe (Head Coach/Debate)</u>   <u>Ms Katy Lovegreen (Interp)</u>
Work:
Cell:
E-mail:

<u>Ms Maria Skala (Speech)</u>
Work:
Cell:
E-mail:

The Season:

We start practice on August 31st and continue throughout the school year, until the culmination of each individual student's year. For most, this means practices will end with the district tournaments in March. (*For those who qualify for state and/or nationals, practices will continue after districts.*)

Practices are held Mondays and Wednesdays after school from 2:10-3:45 in room G204. Speech/interpretation events meet on Mondays, and debate events meet on Wednesdays.

To be eligible for competition, a student must attend 90% of practices for his or her primary event and 50% of practices for secondary events. All absences must be excused by a parent or guardian and coordinated with the coaching staff. (We are more than happy to work with other activities and sports in the school, as well.) If the Monday/Wednesday schedule does not work for you, you may attempt to arrange alternate practice times with Mr Briscoe & Ms Skala.

Tournaments

Each student should plan to compete in every local tournament, although we are willing to work with student needs.

If you are signed up for a tournament, you are expected to be there on time. Failure to appear at a tournament will result in consequences up to and including removal from the team. You may not drop an event less than 4 days before a tournament. Failure to adhere to this policy could result in a 2 tournament suspension for the first offense.

You should observe or help out with timing events when you are not actively competing. In addition, we must know where you are at all times. When you leave/are picked up by your parents, always tell a coach you are leaving. Leaving a tournament early is by exception only and requires parental coordination with the coaching staff prior to the event. Standard practice is that all team members will ride the bus to tournaments.

All South team members will be at the South Tournament, no exceptions. Plan to be here for the entire tournament, including set up and clean up as needed before and after the tournament.

The list below identifies the tournaments we currently have on the schedule for this season.

Date	Tournament	Open/Invitational/Qualifying
Oct. 21-22, '11	South HS, AK	Open (Mandatory)
Oct. 28-29, '11	Bartlett HS, AK	Open
Nov. 11-12, '11	Eagle River HS, AK	Open
Dec. 9-10, '11	Dimond HS, AK	Open
Jan. 20-21, '12	Wasilla HS, AK	Open Invitational
Jan. 27-28, '12	West HS, AK	Open
Feb. 1-6, '12	Golden Desert Invit., Las Vegas, NV	Open Invitational
Feb. 10-11, '12	Service HS, AK	Open
Feb. 16-18, '12	AK State Championships East HS & UAA	Qualifying
May 24-29, '12*	Catholic Forensic League National Championships, Baltimore, MD	Qualifying
Jun. 9-17, '12 *	National Forensic League National Championships, Indianapolis, IN	Qualifying

*Dates are estimated based on travel

Tournament Etiquette

Tournament dress must be business-like. No jeans and t-shirts--think nice pants/skirts/dresses and shirts/blouses. Drama students may wear clothes that are easy to move in, but must still be professional attire.

Do not enter a competition room while another competitor is performing. When entering or leaving a room, be as quiet and respectful as humanly possible. In addition, do not enter a room immediately before or after a South student performs. Watch at least one person on either side of our competitor. You may laugh at a funny performance, but do not be disrespectful by making excessive noise or comments. In fact, do not make comments at all about a performance as it could influence a judge's decision. Applaud for competitors and treat them with the respect you wish to be given during your performances.

When in a team room or competition room, never touch or use items in that teacher's room. We are guests in their classroom.

There is an awards ceremony at the end of each tournament. Hopefully, the South Wolverines will be featured often! Attendance is mandatory for everyone entered in the tournament. At those events, we are always polite and represent our school with dignity. We clap for all award winners, and we never "showboat" when we are successful. In short, act like you've been there before.

The reasoning behind these behaviors is two-fold. First and foremost, they demonstrate respect for ourselves and other individuals. Dressing well sends a statement about how you view yourself. Being respectful of other competitors shows that you value their hard work, dedication, and contributions to the educational aspect of forensics. Refraining from showboating at awards also shows respect for your fellow finalists. Second, engaging in these respectful behaviors—and avoiding the disrespectful ones—ultimately increases our team's ethos. This, in turn, translates to additional success in competition. Make judges want to vote for you…not against you.

Goal Setting

Each student should meet with one of the coaches to set individual goals for each tournament, the competitive year, and his or her forensics career. We will then work out a plan to achieve those goals.

Code of Conduct

These policies serve as an addendum to official school policy and ASAA regulations. If in conflict, the school, district, and ASAA policies take precedence.

1) Alcohol/Drug Use or Influence: Students will refrain from the use of alcohol or other drugs while on forensics tournaments or at team functions. Likewise, students will not report to team activities (practice, tournaments, etc.) under the influence of alcohol or other drugs. The first offense will result in a two-tournament suspension. The second offense will result in expulsion from the team.

2) Sexual Activities: Students will refrain from engaging in sexual activities at all team events. The first offense will result in a two-tournament suspension. The second offense will result in expulsion from the team.

3) Unethical Behavior: Unethical behavior includes such practices as plagiarism, falsifying evidence, distorting evidence, and fabricating sources. The first offense will result in a two-tournament suspension. The second offense will result in expulsion from the team.

A. Examples of plagiarism range from the most severe example of cutting and pasting another's work to be used as your own original material to simply expressing another's ideas in your own words without giving them credit for their analysis and contribution to your work.

B. Examples of distorting evidence include a speaker using a portion of an author's work that disagrees with his or her final conclusions; surrounding a quotation with additional words or phrases, while giving the impression that all of them came from the original source; or simply misusing their ideas to advance your own. *This is different than using a quotation as a starting point for developing your own original thought. If you have a question, ask...*

C. Examples of fabricating sources include making up citations and sources to be used in a speech, using a real quotation while intentionally attributing it to a different author, or paraphrasing an idea you've heard but using a made-up author and date in your speech.

4) Other Thoughts: Specific rules (curfew, attire, meeting times, etc.) may vary depending on the tournament, the location, and the number of students traveling on a particular trip. While traveling on forensics tournaments we are representatives of our families and South Anchorage High School. As such, we will conduct ourselves as the responsible adults we are.

Should you choose to violate any of these policies, both your parent/guardian and an appropriate school administrator will be notified of your unprofessional conduct. For further information on ethics policy please refer to the Code of Ethics on page 1 of the ASAA DDF Handbook. **http://asaa.org/sportsactivities/ddf/pdf/200809ddfhandbook.pdf**

Final Thoughts

DDF Letter (*per the South Anchorage High School Student Handbook*)

1) Participation in more than 50% of all scheduled forensics contests in the local area

2) Individual school placement (1st, 2nd, or 3rd) in at least three contests in the same event
    OR
2) Participation in debate with a winning record (50% win percentage)

District Tournament Eligibility

The state and national organizations have specific eligibility requirements for the district tournament. Those will be our starting point for determining our district teams. In addition, we take into consideration (in no particular order): competitive success, work ethic, contributions to the team, support of the DDF community, and so forth.

National Tournament Eligibility

Students will have the opportunity to qualify to one (or both) of the two major national championship tournaments: the National Catholic Forensic League's Grand National Tournament over Memorial Day Weekend and the National Speech & Debate Association's national championship tournament in June. In the event students qualify to either of these, we will work to ensure they can participate if they are available.

NSDA/NFL Membership/Points

South is a member school of the National Speech & Debate Association (NSDA), the world's largest national honor society recognizing achievement and participation in forensics. Students earn points by competing in tournaments. You can also earn points for participation in Mock Trial, Student Congress, Model UN, speeches of at least 3 minutes in front of at least 25 adults, presentations at high school assemblies, etc.

Once you have earned 25 points, you can become a member of the national honor society for forensics competitors. It should be noted, that many colleges and universities provide additional weight to students' applications when those applicants have been members of the NSDA. In addition, NSDA membership provides opportunities for national level awards, academic achievement scholarships, and so forth.

Service Point Recording Form

Student Name: _____   Date of Speech: _____

Description of Speech & Audience: _____
<small>(Ex: Oratory, Extemporaneous, Emcee, Impromptu, etc.) & (Ex: Rotary, TV, PTA, Church, etc.)</small>

Length of Speech: _____   Approx # Adults: _____
<small>(Min: 3 minutes "on stage"</small>   <small>(Min: 25 adults unless HS assembly)</small>

------------Cut Here--------------------------Cut Here-----------------------Cut Here--------------

Service Point Recording Form

Student Name: _____   Date of Speech: _____

Description of Speech & Audience: _____
<small>(Ex: Oratory, Extemporaneous, Emcee, Impromptu, etc.) & (Ex: Rotary, TV, PTA, Church, etc.)</small>

Length of Speech: _____   Approx # Adults: _____
<small>(Min: 3 minutes "on stage"</small>   <small>(Min: 25 adults unless HS assembly)</small>

------------Cut Here--------------------------Cut Here-----------------------Cut Here--------------

Service Point Recording Form

Student Name: _____   Date of Speech: _____

Description of Speech & Audience: _____
<small>(Ex: Oratory, Extemporaneous, Emcee, Impromptu, etc.) & (Ex: Rotary, TV, PTA, Church, etc.)</small>

Length of Speech: _____   Approx # Adults: _____
<small>(Min: 3 minutes "on stage"</small>   <small>(Min: 25 adults unless HS assembly)</small>

------------Cut Here--------------------------Cut Here-----------------------Cut Here--------------

Service Point Recording Form

Student Name: _____   Date of Speech: _____

Description of Speech & Audience: _____
<small>(Ex: Oratory, Extemporaneous, Emcee, Impromptu, etc.) & (Ex: Rotary, TV, PTA, Church, etc.)</small>

Length of Speech: _____   Approx # Adults: _____
<small>(Min: 3 minutes "on stage"</small>   <small>(Min: 25 adults unless HS assembly)</small>

South Anchorage High DDF Team Contract
2011-12 School Year

I, _____, agree to abide by the rules specified in the South Anchorage High School DDF Team Handbook. I also acknowledge that if I do not comply with any of those rules, I can and will be released from the team and forfeit my ability to compete for the South DDF Team. My signature below also indicates that I have been provided a copy of said DDF Team Handbook.

_____
Printed Name of Student

_____
Signature of Student

_____
Date

_____
Printed Name of Parent/Guardian

_____
Signature of Parent/Guardian

_____
Date

Parent Involvement

Early in the season you should get your students' caregiver(s) involved. Having dedicated adults can make your job easier, provide the students with additional opportunities, and provide a source of future support in your interactions with administrators and school boards. At a minimum hold an early season meeting for parents and guardians that can serve as both a recruiting tool and an introduction to the team.

Sample Parents' Meeting Flyer

TALKING RAMS PARENT MEETING

Thursday, September 8th – 7:00 PM – Cafeteria

Questions? - Contact Molly Beck, Head Coach, at mbeck@ladueschools.net

Parent Support and Involvement Form

Name(s): _____

Son(s)/Daughter(s): _____

E-mail Address(es): _____

Phone Number(s): _____

Please place a checkmark next to areas of interest:

_____ Manage the hospitality room and staff at our annual tournament

_____ Make a financial contribution for the hospitality room at our annual tournament

_____ Provide food/snacks for the team during tournaments

_____ Make a financial contribution to the senior scholarship fund

_____ Make a financial contribution to the speech and debate camp scholarship fund

_____ Make a financial contribution to support out-of-area travel for our team

_____ Contact your employer about providing financial support or sponsorship

_____ Help plan the team banquet and organize the dinner

_____ Serve as host for team social and/or awards events

_____ Serve as a judge at local tournaments

_____ Serve as a chaperone on out-of-area travel

_____ Provide a list of possible guest speakers/presenters and contact information to the head coach

_____ Serve as a volunteer coach

Thank you for your willingness to actively support our students!

Team Events and Tournament Permission Slip

I, _____, give my son/daughter, _____, permission to attend and/or compete in the following in-town regular season team events and tournaments:

GSL Pre-Season Festival	17 September 2016	Mehlville High School
Oakville Autumn Congress	01 October 2016	Oakville High School
Parkway West Invitational	14-15 October 2016	Parkway West High School
GSL Conference Tournament #1	21-22 October 2016	Liberty High School (Wentzville)
Francis Howell North Events Round Robin	04 November 2016	Francis Howell North High School
Francis Howell Central Debate Round Robin	05 November 2016	Francis Howell Central High School
GSL Conference Tournament #2	11-12 November 2016	Brentwood High School
Ladue Novice Invitational	18-19 November 2016	Ladue Middle School
Randy Pierce Winter Classic	09-10 December 2016	Pattonville High School
Oakville Novice Events Round Robin	06 January 2017	Oakville High School
Parkway Central Novice Debate Round Robin	07 January 2017	Parkway Central High School
GSL Conference Tournament #3	21-22 January 2017	Ritenour High School
Marquette Invitational	17-18 February 2017	Marquette High School

I understand that granting permission only means my son/daughter has permission to attend the event and that I will have an opportunity to discuss participation in each event on a case-by-case basis before tournament registration is due. I also understand that all out-of-town trips, district tournaments, the state tournament, and national tournaments will require an additional permission slip.

_____   _____
Parent Signature   Date

_____
Printed Name

_____   _____
Parent Signature   Date

_____
Printed Name

Events Guide

Providing an event guide like the one on the following pages can be very helpful for two groups of people. First, it can be distributed at your team's annual recruiting drive or meeting. This allows students a chance to read about the various events offered by your team, which can help them decide on what events they want to participate in during the upcoming season. Second, it can be distributed to new judges. Many volunteer judges are apprehensive about judging or are unsure about what the activity is. A simple synopsis of the events helps them understand why the events exist and helps them provide meaningful comments when they fill out ballots.

Limited Preparation Speaking Events
(aka- Extemporaneous Speaking)

Description
  These events require competitors to have an in-depth understanding of current events that allows them to formulate an original synthesis of the topic. It tasks the individual to prepare a 7-minute speech in 30 minutes (from choosing a topic, to organizing a speech, to practicing it). Competitors are given three questions from which to choose. Hence, the event focuses on critical thinking and public speaking in a taxing environment.

Long-term Benefits
  Develop the skills needed in classes using a seminar format
  Enhance paper writing skills
  Hone public speaking skills
  Enhance knowledge of current events
  Heighten comprehension of popular media, as well as college- and graduate-level material

Things to Look for as a Judge
  Does the student directly (and clearly) answer the question?
  Does the competitor's answer make logical sense?
      - This does not mean you agree with his or her conclusions
  Is the competitor's answer supported with research, quotations, statistics from credible
      sources?
  Does the student provide a useful introduction and conclusion?
      - Attention-getter, restate the question, answer the question/thesis, wrap-up, etc.
  Does the competitor deliver the speech effectively?
      - Fluency, pronunciation, gestures, nonverbals, eloquence, etc.
      - Provides a clear intro, body, and conclusion

Types of Extemp
  United States Extemp (USX) or Domestic Extemp (DX)
      - Questions specifically related to the United States
  International Extemp (IX) or Foreign Extemp (FX)
      - Questions related to foreign affairs with a global focus

Platform Speaking Events

Original Oratory

Description

Competitors present a pre-prepared speech from memory. The focus is on thought, composition, and delivery. The primary goal is to communicate effectively through speech communication. Thus, an effective delivery is paramount. The thought and composition competitors put into their speech serve mainly to aid the delivery. The topic should be both interesting and thoughtful. A simple informative speech generally does not do as well in this event. Rather, speeches should be geared towards persuasion. Examples can include: alerting the audience to a potential danger, strengthening devotion to a cause, or encouraging the audience to take future action. Rhetoric and diction are very important in this event.

Long-term Benefits
Enhance paper writing skills
Hone public speaking skills

Things to Look for as a Judge
Does the student provide a clear thesis?
Does the competitor present a topic of relevance/significance (or attempt to explain why the topic is significant)?
Does the competitor's argument make logical sense?
- This does not mean you agree with his or her conclusions
Is the competitor's answer supported with research, quotations, statistics from credible sources?
Does the student provide a useful introduction and conclusion?
- Attention-getter, clear and focused thesis statement, wrap-up, etc.
Does the competitor deliver the speech effectively?
- Fluency, pronunciation, gestures, nonverbals, eloquence, etc.
- Provides a clear intro, body, and conclusion

Expository or Informative Speaking

Description
This is very similar to Original Oratory; however, speeches tend to be more informative in nature. Students are also allowed to use visual aids.

Long-term Benefits
Enhance paper writing skills
Hone public speaking skills

Things to Look for as a Judge
Does the student provide a clear thesis?
Does the competitor's speech effectively inform the audience about a topic?
Does the competitor use visual aids effectively? (*Some leagues allow one or more visual aids.*)
Does the student provide a useful introduction and conclusion?
- Attention-getter, thesis statement, wrap-up, etc.
Does the competitor deliver the speech effectively?
- Fluency, pronunciation, gestures, nonverbals, eloquence, etc.

Interpretation of Literature Events

Description
  Competitors recreate the characters in a published story, making them seem living and real to the audience. The piece must be memorized. The presentation must be devoid of props, in any form. Movement around the room should be kept to a minimum. (*Some leagues require students to remain within an imaginary 3-foot x 3-foot box for one-person events or 6-foot x 6-foot for Duo Interp.*) Examples of the types of pieces that may be "cut" into an interp: novels, short stories, plays, comic books, screenplays, poems, and so forth. The literary merit is judged, in addition to the actual performance. Contestants are also evaluated on their poise, quality and use of voice, inflections, emphasis, pronunciation, enunciation, physical expression, and the ability to interpret multiple characters correctly and consistently. The audience should feel as though it is watching the story unfold in real life. The audience should also gain a clear understanding of what the piece means to the individual performer.

Long-term Benefits
  Develop an appreciation for and understanding of literature
  Enhance acting abilities
  Understand how body language, tone of voice, movement, etc. impact communication

Things to Look for as a Judge
  Does the student deliver the piece from memory without stumbling?
  Does the selected piece have literary merit and/or social significance?
      - Does the student's interpretation (meaning or understanding) of the piece shine
          through?
  Does the competitor make you believe they are the character(s) they are playing…
          despite not being allowed to use props and costumes?
      - In other words, do they demonstrate acting ability?
  Generally, more technical pieces (multiple characters, difficult settings) are regarded
          more highly than less technical pieces.

Types of Interpretation
  Dramatic Interp (DI)
      - Pieces are dramatic in nature… "dramatic" does not necessarily mean "sad"
  Humorous Interp (HI)
      - Pieces are humorous in nature
      - While a humorous piece is good, the primary focus is on judging the
          competitor's ability to make the piece humorous
  Duo Interp (Duo)
      - Performed with a partner (2 people)
      - Either humorous or dramatic
      - Competitors may not make physical or eye contact with one another

Debate Events

<u>Things to Look for as a Judge</u>
Do the debaters present sound, logical arguments?
- This does not mean you agree with his or her conclusions
- This question has to do with how well they build and counter each other's arguments
- Debaters are supposed to debate each other's arguments, not the judge's thoughts
Do the debaters use research, quotations, statistics, anecdotes, analogies, analysis, etc., to make their point?
Note: Never judge a debate event based on whether or not you agree with the debater. Your task is to evaluate his or her argumentation relative to that of the opponent(s). In fact, in most debate formats, the students do not get to choose their side…it is assigned to them a few minutes before the start of the round.

Policy Debate
<u>Description</u>
This is a team event, consisting of two people. The focus of the event is on Analysis, Argumentation, Refutation, Adaptation, and Organization. Arguments are rooted heavily in the area of study referred to as political science. Competitors debate the same topic all year; however, the specifics of each round can vary substantially.

<u>Long-term Benefits</u>
Ability to quickly develop a coherent argument in support of your position
Ability to quickly identify the flaw's in another person's argument
Develop organizational skills
Gain knowledge in the fields of social sciences, political science, behavioral science, government, international relations, inter-cultural relations, economics, etc.
Enhance comprehension of popular media, as well as college- and graduate-level material
Develop research skills
Develop the skills needed in classes using a seminar format

<u>Recent Policy Topics:</u>
Resolved: The United States federal government should substantially increase its non-military exploration and/or development of the Earth's oceans.
Resolved: The United States federal government should substantially curtail its domestic surveillance.
Resolved: The United States federal government should substantially increase its economic and/or diplomatic engagement with the People's Republic of China.
Resolved: The United States federal government should substantially increase its funding and/or regulation of elementary and/or secondary education in the United States.

Key Issues the Affirmative and Negative May Debate About

1. Is there a need for the affirmative?
  - Does the affirmative demonstrate a problem (something bad) with the present system?
  - Does the affirmative demonstrate that the system has failed to properly fix the problem?
2. The affirmative should advocate a solution that falls within the bounds of the debate topic.
3. Does the affirmative lead to more good than bad? (Yes, vote Aff. No, vote Neg.)
  - Does the affirmative demonstrate that their proposal (aka- plan) reduces the problem?
  - The affirmative may provide other reasons or examples of how its plan does good things.
  - The negative should provide reasons why the affirmative plan leads to "bad things"
    -- Does the negative demonstrate disadvantages of adopting the plan?
    -- Does the negative present an alternative (aka- counterplan) that is better than the plan?
    -- Does the negative demonstrate that the affirmative uses flawed reasoning, which causes bad things to happen?

Lincoln-Douglas Debate

Description

   This format of debate is a one-on-one event. Rather than debating specific policies, this form of debate focuses on the values behind our choices. In other words, it encourages competitors to look at and challenge the assumptions behind our decisions. Arguments are rooted heavily in philosophy. Competitors debate a different topic every two months. Emphasis is balanced between delivery and philosophical analysis of the topic area.

Long-term Benefits
  Learn to challenge the assumptions behind another person's framework of thought
  Ability to understand the nature of our world, society, species
  Explore philosophy (Aristotle, Kant, Mill, Marx, etc.)
  Enhance comprehension of popular media, as well as college- and graduate-level material

Recent Lincoln Douglas Topics:
Resolved: Immigration ought to be recognized as a human right.
Resolved: Countries ought to prohibit the production of nuclear power.
Resolved: The United States ought to limit qualified immunity for policy officers.
Resolved: Public colleges and universities in the United States ought not restrict any constitutionally protected speech.
Resolved: The United States ought to guarantee the right to housing.

<u>Key Elements</u>
Both Affirmative and Negative debaters should present an overarching value they believe is of primary importance. This becomes the standard by which the round should be evaluated.

Examples of Values include: Justice, Fairness, Utilitarianism, Equality

Both the Affirmative and Negative should present a criterion for determining whether affirmation or negation of the resolution achieves the value in question.

Examples of Criteria include: Rule of Law, Education, Equality of Opportunity

Often, a criterion is a stepping stone to the value. For example, a debater might argue that we cannot have a "Just" society (the value) if we do not abide by the "Rule of Law" (the criteria).

Public Forum
<u>Description</u>
This is a team event, consisting of two people. Discussions focus on current events and change monthly. The event is not technical and is judged primarily on a team's presentation of arguments in a persuasive manner. The ability to frame a controversial topic in a clear and compelling manner is critical. The event was originally modeled after shows like Crossfire and The O'Reilly Factor. The purpose of the event was to minimize technical debate in an effort to develop the skills needed to quickly persuade a typical person in society.

<u>Recent Public Forum Topics:</u>
Resolved: On balance, the benefits of the Internet of Things outweigh the harms of decreased personal privacy.
Resolved: The United States should end Plan Columbia.
Resolved: The United States should lift its embargo against Cuba.
Resolved: The United States should no longer pressure Israel to work toward a two-state solution.
Resolved: The United States ought to replace the Electoral College with a direct national popular vote.

Congressional Debate/Student Congress
<u>Description</u>
In this event, students are assigned to chambers consisting of 10-30 students. Each member of the chamber (including the Presiding Officer) is competing against everyone else. Debates usually focus on current events and follow basic standards of parliamentary procedure, as you might find in congress. The event is not intended to be technical. Ultimately, the goal of every member of the chamber is to make the debate better and to advance our understanding of the issue being debated.

<u>Topics:</u>
Varied. Students are given the legislative docket 1-2 weeks prior to the tournament.

Individual Goals Survey

1. Why did you join the Speech & Debate team?

2. What event(s) do you plan to participate in?

3. Why did you choose that (those) event(s)?

4. Identify your short-term (this year) speech & debate/forensics goals.

5. Identify your long-term (next year, etc.) speech & debate/forensics goals.

Student Leadership

Strong programs utilize student leaders to promote the development of their programs. Whether you identify team captains, event coordinators, or student leaders, it is important to use them in effective ways. In effect, they should be assistant coaches.

For example, Shawn historically holds elections for club positions (President, Vice President, Secretary, Treasurer, etc.) Those students are responsible for organizing social functions, ensuring the team is represented throughout the school (pep rallies, morning announcements, locker decorations, student government, etc.), spearheading fundraising opportunities, and so forth. The coaches identify event specific captains (Policy Captain, Lincoln Douglas Captain, Extemp Captain, Interp Captain, etc.) Those students are responsible for assisting with practice. In the event the coaching staff organizes a lesson or practice for debaters, the Speech and Interp Captains organize lessons for students that compete solely in those events. If the coaching staff holds a practice exclusively for policy debaters, the Lincoln Douglas Captain might lead a discussion on the new LD topic while the Interp Captain might critique pieces of other students. In this way, the students serve as coaches and significantly add to the growth of the team.

As another example, Molly created a formal selection process for team leaders with clearly identified responsibilities. Her team leadership consists of Officers and Coordinators. Those students wishing to serve as Officers submit a brief resume and candidacy statement. The candidate statements are forwarded to the entire team. Finally, all team members have the opportunity to vote for next year's Officers. Those students wishing to serve as Coordinators submit an application to and are interviewed by a selection team. The selection team is comprised of multiple individuals to include the coach and a combination of people such as, the outgoing Coordinators, alumni, and/or coaches at other schools. The eligibility and responsibility guidelines can be found on the following pages.

Team Leadership
Expectations

- Attend one training session and/or planning meeting at the end of the Spring 2017 semester
- Complete all duties in a timely manner
- Attend events as needed (Open House, Parent Meetings, etc.)
- Assist in promoting the speech and debate team
- Work at the Ladue Novice Invitational
- Stay for the awards ceremony at each tournament regardless of personal results
- Maintain a 3.0 average and receive S or O for all citizenship ratings
- No behavior/discipline issues
- Attend officer or coordinator meetings
- Set a positive example for all team members – at school, during practice, and at tournaments (in and out of rounds)
- Remember leadership role at all times
- Cooperate with coaches on all matters concerning the Talking Rams
- Enroll in the Forensics class
- Compete or judge at all tournaments unless a valid excuse is presented to coaches

Officer Positions

President
Seniors only
- Preside over officer and team meetings
- Represent the speech and debate team at events and meetings
- Mentor and hold other officers accountable
- Work with the head coach to develop a leadership development program for officers
- Apply for the National Speech & Debate Association (NSDA) student leadership organization

Vice President
Juniors and seniors only
- Serve as student leader of NSDA
- Organize end-of-year awards ceremony with coaches
- Track NFL points with coaches – create visual representation of points and recognize advance degrees
- Track NFL points for judging and other non-tournament events (mock trial, etc.)
- Assist the president in representing the speech and debate team at events and meetings

Director of Recruitment
Sophomores and juniors only
- Work with team members and middle school teachers to identify and reach out to potential freshmen members
- Coordinate the 4th quarter middle school speech and debate club
- Work with team members and high school teachers to identify and reach out to potential team members
- Represent the team at the high school activity fair in the Fall semester
- Coordinate PR efforts at the beginning of the school year to recruit members

Director of Membership Development
Sophomores and juniors only
- Create a buddy/mentor system for novices
- Organize team dinners after team events/tournaments
- Provide opportunities for bonding and team building
- Organize a sendoff for seniors
- Work with the head coach and other officers to develop a member recognition program

Director of Administration
Open to all grade levels
- Write thank you notes to schools hosting tournaments/events
- Develop a monthly newsletter to send to parents and team members
- Assist in keeping membership records for team members
- Serve as Historian for the team – ensure pictures are taken are team events, collect any news about the team, create a slideshow for the end of the year, etc.
- Develop and carry out a PR plan for the team

Coordinator Expectations

General
Seniors and/or juniors only

- Turn in lesson plans and handouts a minimum of 24 hours in advance
- Develop a long-term practice plan to ensure growth and development of team members
- Meet with coaches regularly to assess the growth and development of team members
- Communicate issues in the event to coaches
- Conference with team members after tournaments
- Check in with team members before and after rounds
- Set an example by practicing with coaches regularly
- Meet all competition material deadlines
- Ensure practices are beneficial and effective for team members
- Delegate teaching and leading responsibilities to varsity members
- Inform coaches if team members are not ready to compete at a specific tournament

Debate

- Coordinate evidence briefs
- Set timelines for case development and hold members accountable
- Develop a practice schedule before each tournament
- Provide sample cases for novices before the first tournament
- Review cases before practice rounds

Speech & Interp Events

- Coordinate files and team resources
- Set timelines for development of pieces/files/etc. and hold members accountable
- Develop a practice schedule for each tournament
- Provide samples for novices
- Review competition materials before tournaments

Assistant Coordinators
Sophomores and/or juniors only

- Shadow your assigned coordinator to gain an understanding of the role
- Complete tasks delegated to you
- Assist in teaching and organizing your assigned event
- Review competition materials
- Conference with your assigned coordinator regularly

Service

Most coaches define their teams through one of two missions: education or competition. While we believe the educational goals should be paramount due to the focus on the students' well-being, there are other considerations, as well. Every program should seek to incorporate some element of service. In addition to altruistic motivations, this aspect of your program offers many benefits for the program to include recruiting new students, generating outside support for the program, fostering a sense of citizenship in students, and developing competitors' skills.

While it's tempting to be like every other club by supporting school activities (decorating the gym for a school dance) or the community (participating in a food drive), we think there is much our teams have to offer through speech and debate as an activity. Here are three ways in which a speech and debate team can serve the community by embracing its inherent talent.

Start a Middle School Speech & Debate Program: Work with a local middle school (or schools) to develop a competitive speech and debate program. Define the scope of the program by the size and interests of your own team. Do not feel compelled to offer the full range of events. Choose a single type of debate with a series of competitions over the course of the year, organize a single platform speaking contest, and/or help English teachers explore literature in their classroom through interpretation of literature. Regardless of the scope of events or type of competitive environment offered, you will energize future high school competitors, build allies amongst faculty members in your district, and develop your own students' skills as they serve as educators and judges for younger students.

Host an Intramural Tournament: Have your students serve as coaches, judges, and tournament staff during an intramural competition. Many students are reluctant to join the speech and debate team for a myriad of reasons. However, they might be willing to participate in a single event rather than committing to an entire year. Obviously, this contest could offer the full spectrum of competitive speech and debate events. Alternatively, you could hold an Intramural Student Congress or use the World Schools Debate format for a single day or after school competition. Again, this type of service can pay dividends as you spark the interest of potential new recruits, enhance your students' skills by making them the educators, and help your administration see that your program benefits the entire school.

Build Partnerships with the District/School: Keep abreast of topics that will be discussed at school board meetings and, in some cases, faculty meetings. Offer to introduce a controversial topic through a debate. A modified World Schools Debate format works well for this type of setting. (Have four students present the topic with 4- or 5-minute speeches: 1st Pro, 1st Con, 2nd Pro, 2nd Con. Allow the use of Points of Information. Thus, the debate can be completed in 16-20 minutes.) Such introductory debates amaze administrators, teachers, and community members. They begin to see the true value in our activity. Often, your students' arguments and framing of the topic serve as the springboard for the discussion that follows and are referenced by those who speak formally on the subject. (*Be tenacious. Do not take "no" for an answer. At first, the school board/administration is unlikely to give your team the floor through this type of environment. They will likely balk at the amount of time requested and either decline your offer or ask you to do something in 2-4 minutes. Politely decline until you can do something that showcases your team AND provides meaningful support to the organization. Keep circling back to your original request. Ask the superintendent or principal for a private demonstration. Give them to a chance to see your vision in action.*)

Tournaments

Navigating Tournaments

The first tournament can be a daunting experience for many competitors. For those who have never attended a speech and debate contest, simple things like reading the postings (also known as schematics and pairings) might induce anxiety. As coaches, we can minimize the fear of the unknown by introducing students to the tournament experience before they ever travel to the first competition sight. The following Tournament Scavenger Hunt and Novice Practice Tournament provide them that experience.

Tournament Scavenger Hunt

To help ensure students arrive at the location they are supposed to doing tournaments, you should introduce them to the process of reading the postings and navigating a tournament location.

Preparation

1. Create postings for a fictional tournament that incorporates rooms from your own building. Be sure to coordinate with other teachers if accessing classrooms is limited during your practice times. Alternatively, you may be able to use common areas such as the library, cafeteria, gymnasium, faculty lounge, etc.) *See example posting: Forensic Scavenger Hunt – Round 1.*

2. Prepare photo scavenger hunt instructions for each section. Be sure to use common items that are likely to be found in the rooms you use for the activity. Hang the instructions on the door to each room. *See example instructions: Forensic Scavenger Hunt Treasure List. (If you have students without phones, just have them write down what they were supposed to find. To ensure your students found the correct room, be sure to create a separate treasure list for every section.)*

Procedure

1. Assign each student a code from the fictional pairing. As an extension, you may wish to assign experienced competitors to a group of novice students to serve as their "coach" for the activity. The coach can provide assistance and evaluate whether the "contestants" were successful in their quests.

2. Inform students that they will mimic the process of attending an actual tournament through a photo scavenger hunt. This will be a two-round tournament, in which they have been assigned a speaker code. When the postings go up, they will need to find their code and determine their assigned room and speaker order. They are to proceed to their assigned room and follow the instructions that have been posted on the door to the classroom.

3. Post the Round 1 Pairings. For added realism, identify a common posting area such as the cafeteria.

4. After students return from the first round, post the Round 2 Pairings.

Forensic Scavenger Hunt
Events - Round 1

Section 1 G102	Section 2 H203	Section 3 Library
10A	3B	9C
2B	1A	4B
4A	2A	13C
25A	14B	2C
1B	10B	8A
13A	25B	14A

Forensic Scavenger Hunt
Debate - Round 1

	Aff	Neg
G201	3B	9C
G103	1A	4A
H202	2A	13C
H105	14B	2C

Forensic Scavenger Hunt
Events - Round _____

Section 1	Section 2	Section 3

Forensic Scavenger Hunt
Debate - Round _____

	Aff	Neg

Forensic Scavenger Hunt Treasure List
Events - Round 1, Section 1

Instructions: Referencing your assigned speaker order, use your phone to take a picture of the item listed. Then, return to the postings area to report your findings to your coach.

First Speaker – Teacher's desk

Second Speaker – Clock

Third Speaker – Any Textbook

Fourth Speaker – Student desk

Fifth Speaker – Room Number Placard (in hallway)

Sixth Speaker – Poster or Bulletin Board

Forensic Scavenger Hunt Treasure List
Debate - Round 1, Section 1

Instructions: Referencing your assigned side, use your phone to take a picture of the item listed. Then, return to the postings area to report your findings to your coach.

Affirmative Team – Bookshelf

Negative Team – Intercom Speaker

Novice Practice Tournament

A few weeks prior to the first competition, host a novice practice tournament that introduces students to the complete tournament experience using easily accessible events. It also allows varsity members to get experience judging and the student leaders/captains gain experience hosting a tournament and providing leadership and guidance for the team.

Events Offered:

Duet Improvisational Acting
Impromptu Speaking
Extemporaneous Debate

Obviously, you can do this activity with any number of events. We choose to focus on three limited preparation events that are relatively accessible and fun for incoming members. The benefit of using these events is that you cover debate, public speaking, and interpretation so students can apply the skills used for these events to the main events team members will compete in throughout the year.

Event Descriptions:

Duet Improvisational Acting
- Students draw three prompts thirty minutes before their performance and choose one
- Students have thirty minutes to prepare a seven-minute scene based on the prompt
- Prompts are written by the student leaders and/or coaches

Impromptu Speaking
- Students draw three prompts five minutes before their performance time and choose one
- Students have five minutes to prepare a five-minute speech
- Topics are prepared by student leaders and/or coaches

Extemporaneous Debate
- Utilize the National Speech and Debate Association rules and structure (speechanddebate.org)
- Resolutions are written by student leaders and/or coaches

Tournament Structure:

MONDAY

Event: Duet Improvisational Acting

Rationale: This is a partner event so it is less intimidating for new students. The prompts are usually fun and the interpretation events draw people in quickly. It is a great way to kick off the week.

Procedure:
- The student leaders for Interpretation Events instruct novices and team members on the structure and rules and offer general advice
- Two varsity members, who have previously prepped, perform their scene
- Student leaders for Interpretation Events offer constructive feedback – this is key because it starts to make the feedback process a team norm for all team members
- While the varsity members are providing instruction and demonstrations, novices are divided into pairs and given a code, and a schedule is created
- The codes area assigned and the schedules are posted
- Draw begins and partners have thirty minutes to prepare their scenes
  - It is helpful to have experienced Extemporaneous Speaking competitors run draw for this event to help make the draw experience as realistic as possible
- Varsity members are assigned to judge rounds and complete ballots to provide constructive feedback
  - After the round, a senior or junior with judging experience reviews the ballots to make sure they are good ballots (constructive, not too harsh, etc.)
- At the end of the performances, the competitors in that room vote for their favorite performance (no team may vote for themselves) and the winning team gets a small prize (candy, gift card, etc.)
- Debriefing is done after the final performance with an experienced upperclassman facilitating the conversation

TUESDAY

Event: Impromptu Speaking

Rationale: Students are often hesitant about this event, so doing it after Duet Improvisational Acting gets students to come back for Impromptu Speaking.

Procedure:
- The student leaders for Extemporaneous Speaking instruct novices and team members on the structure and rules and offer general advice
- One varsity member gives a sample speech
  - It is helpful to have this student prep on a dry erase board so novices can see the preparation process in action
- Student leaders for Extemporaneous Speaking offer constructive feedback – this is key because it starts to make the feedback process a team norm for all team members
- While the varsity members are providing instruction and demonstrations, novices are given a code and a schedule is created
- The codes area assigned and the schedules are posted
- Varsity members are assigned to judge rounds and complete ballots to provide constructive feedback
  - After the round, a senior or junior with judging experience reviews the ballots to make sure they are good ballots (constructive, not too harsh, etc.)
- At the end of the performances, the competitors in that room vote for their favorite speech (no individual may vote for herself/himself) and the winner gets a small prize (candy, gift card, etc.)
- Debriefing is done after the final speech with an experienced upperclassman facilitating the conversation

WEDNESDAY

Event: Extemporaneous Debate

Rationale: As another event that leads to apprehension and one that takes two days to complete, if fits nicely after the other two events.

Procedure:
- The student leaders for Debate instruct novices and team members on the structure and rules and offer some general advice
- Two varsity members compete in a round
  - The NSDA permits students to receive assistance when prepping topics – allow coaches and students to work together while preparing for the example debate
- Student leaders for debate offer constructive feedback – this is key because it starts to make the feedback process a team norm for all team members
- While the varsity members are providing instruction and demonstrations, novices are given a code and a bracket is created
- The codes area assigned and the schedules are posted
- A topic is posted and students split into groups for an hour of prep – varsity students mentor the groups
  - Note: Students should prep both sides of the topic
- Students then go home and are permitted to continue working on their cases and research but are not required to do so

THURSDAY

Event: Extemporaneous Debate (continued)

- Varsity members are assigned to judge rounds and complete ballots to provide constructive feedback
- Students continue moving through the bracket with a coin toss to determine sides for each round
- Everyone judges the final round – varsity and novice members – and the winner gets a small prize (candy, a gift card, etc.)
- After the rounds, a senior or junior with judging experience reviews the ballots to make sure they are good ballots (constructive, not too harsh, etc.)
- Debriefing is done after the final round with an experienced upperclassman facilitating the conversation

Pre-/Post-Tournament Survey

Name: _____

Tournament: _____   Event(s): _____

My pre-tournament goal:

Goal Reflection:

My thoughts on this tournament:

Post-tournament action items:

Trip Sheets

Keeping students, parents, and coaches on the same page is a critical component of headache-free weekends. Before every tournament, I provide students with two copies of a trip sheet that contains important information about the upcoming weekend. One copy is for the students to give to their parents/guardians. This lets the parents know you are taking care of their kids, minimizes their concerns about the weekend, and helps them to understand what is going on throughout the event. The second copy is for the students to bring with them to the tournament itself. This ensures that the coaching staff does not get peppered with a constant barrage of questions: What time is round one? When do we get home? How many sets of competition attire do we need to bring? How many preliminary rounds do we have?

I have two different templates that I use for tournaments. The first is for tournaments in the local area. (The first page is a signup sheet for the tournament. I give them two copies of the second page as the official trip sheet.) The second version of the trip sheet is for when we travel out of the local area.

Bartlett HS
Forensics Tournament Sign Up
October 28-29, 2011

Student Name: _____

Students may enter a maximum of 3 events.
- Students may only enter 1 event during the "Debate Pattern"
- Students may enter no more than 2 events in a single pattern of IEs

In the **<u>debate pattern</u>**, I plan to compete in (*circle one*): Policy   LD   PF

My debate partner is: _____

In **<u>Pattern A</u>**, I would like to compete in (*circle no more than two events*):

Original Oratory   Expository Speaking   Congress

Readers' Theater (List partners: _____)

In **<u>Pattern B</u>**, I would like to compete in (*circle no more than two events*):

Domestic Extemp   Foreign Extemp

Extemporaneous Commentary

Humorous Interpretation   Dramatic Interpretation

Duo Interpretation (Partner: _____)

Bartlett HS
Tournament Schedule
October 28-29, 2011

Friday

10:45	Meet at SAHS (gym entrance)
10:50	Depart SAHS for Bartlett HS
11:30	Arrive at Bartlett HS
11:30-12:30	Registration
12:30-1:45	Pattern A
1:45-3:15	Debate Rd 1
3:30-5:00	Pattern B
5:15-6:45	Debate Rd 2
6:45-8:15	Pattern A Finals
8:15	Depart Bartlett HS
~8:50	Arrive at SAHS (gym entrance)

Saturday

7:45	Meet at SAHS (gym entrance)
7:50	Depart SAHS for Bartlett HS
8:30	Arrive at Bartlett HS
9:00-10:30	Debate Rd 3
10:30-12:00	Pattern B Finals
12:00-1:30	Debate Quarterfinals (or Rd 4)
1:30-3:00	Debate Semifinals
3:00-4:30	Debate Finals
4:00 (ASAP)	Awards
5:00	Depart Bartlett HS
~5:40	Arrive at SAHS (gym entrance)

Urban Debate National Championship
Loyola University & Corboy Law Center, Chicago, IL
April 20-24, 2017

SLUDL
TRIP SHEET

| Please read this trip sheet *carefully* and **bring a copy of it with you to the tournament**. |

To Chicago

We will meet at the **Amtrak – St. Louis – Gateway Station** near the Civic Center Metrolink Station and Scottrade Center at **5:40 am on Thursday, April 20th**. We will depart on Train 302 at 6:40 am with a 12:20 pm arrival at Chicago Union Station. (*Please bring a valid photo ID card. A student ID is sufficient.*)

Return to St Louis

We will depart Chicago on Monday, April 24th, at 7:00 am, arriving in St Louis at 12:20 pm on Train 301. *Students/families will be responsible for getting themselves home.*

Please plan for three days of tournament clothes. Amtrak allows each passenger to bring two personal items and two carry on bags (average size suitcases). However, we will take the L and walk (or use Uber) when we arrive in Chicago, so please pack accordingly.

We are staying at the Hampton Inn Downtown/Magnificent Mile.
Address: 160 E. Huron St, Chicago, IL; Phone: (312) 706-0888

The tournament hotel and competition sites are within walking distance (1/2 mile).
SLUDL may use mass transit, taxis, or shuttles for other team events that are not part of the formal program. *Pack the appropriate footwear for wandering around campus and the city.*

NAUDL/SLUDL will cover student meals directly or through per diem. Students may want to bring extra money for snacks, supplies, and souvenirs.

| Mr Briscoe's Cell: (xxx) xxx-xxxx |

Urban Debate Championship Schedule

Thursday, April 20th
5:40	Meet at Amtrak – Gateway Station
6:40	Depart St. Louis for Chicago on Train 302
12:20	Arrive at Chicago – Union Station
****	Lunch
****	Prep/Explore Chicago/Homework
****	Team Dinner

Friday, April 21st
****	Prep
TBA	Team Photos
3:30	Arrive at Loyola (Water Tower Campus)
4:00	Opening Assembly
4:45	Pairings for Rounds 1 & 2 Released
5:00	Round 1 (Corboy Law Center)
6:30	Pizza dinner (Water Tower Campus)
7:15	Round 2 (Corboy Law Center)

Saturday, April 22nd
6:30	Breakfast at Hampton
7:00	Rd 3 & 4 Pairings Released
8:00	Round 3 (Corboy Law Center)
10:30	Round 4
12:30	Lunch
1:30	Round 5
4:15	Round 6
6:30	Networking Social & Awards (Location TBD)

Sunday, April 23rd
6:30	Breakfast at Hampton
7:00	Pairings released
8:15	Octafinals (Corboy Law Center)
*9:00-3:00	(Optional) "The Insider's Tour of Chicago"
11:00	Quarterfinals
12:30	Lunch
1:45	Semifinals
4:30	Finals
6:30	Trophy presentation to finalists

Monday, April 24th
7:00	Depart Chicago – Union Station on Amtrak Train 301
12:20	Arrive at St. Louis – Gateway Station

Tournament Arrival

When you get to a tournament, the first thing you should do is get your team settled someplace. Find a good location where your team will regroup after every round. Next, get a feel for where the tournament will be located. If the host has told you what rooms are going to be used or what buildings on campus will be used, take a moment to familiarize yourself with the venue. Once you have taken care of your team, it is time to make sure you respect those who have given you access to their space in order for you to take part in the tournament. (*See "Respecting Spaces."*)

Respecting Spaces

As coaches, we want our students to be respectful of the hosts who opened their buildings to us for competition. Obviously, we already talk to our students about keeping our hands off electronic equipment, not taking the teachers' supplies, and picking up our trash. One thing that often goes overlooked is that debaters use the space in a classroom to suit our academic and competitive needs, just as the classroom teacher has her room organized to best suit the needs of her class. One of the most common complaints from teachers and administrators, following a tournament, is that the desks were left in "disarray." While it is more likely that they were left in a configuration that suits a debate or interpretation round, the point is that we should teach our students to respect the space.

Here are two quick things that every student can do to show respect to the hosts:

1) Desk Arrangement: Pull out the cell phone and take a picture of the room when you enter Round 1. At the completion of preliminary rounds, return to that room and put the desks back in the order you found them at the start of the day. (*If you don't have a cellphone, an alternative method is to pull out pen & paper, and quickly sketch the desk layout.*)

2) A Thank You Goes a Long Way: During my time coaching in Alaska, I picked up this idea from the students themselves. While waiting in a classroom for a round to begin, grab a piece of chalk or whiteboard marker, and write a quick thank you on the board. (*BEWARE the SMARTBOARD!*) "Mrs. Hicks – Thank you for letting us use your room for the debate tournament!" Sign your name. (Bonus: In each subsequent round, students should add their names to the board anytime they move to a new room.) (*Mega Bonus: Comment on something cool or unexpected about the teacher's room: "I love your Star Wars posters!" "Go Sooners! I'm applying to OU, too!" "I love how your students decorated the ceiling tiles!"*)

Post Tournament Practice

The first practice following a tournament can be a stressful and confusing time for many students, teams, and coaches. I usually plan to do four things during these practice sessions.

First, get a trip report from one of the students. Select a student to recap the weekend for the entire team. Obviously, there will be the competitive element, highlighting any achievements or success stories. But they should also be free to share stories about the weekend…what happened that made them laugh, made them really think, or inspired them.

Second, let them debrief and decompress. Have a team wide discussion about anything that bothered them or threw them for a loop during the tournament. These discussions could range from arguments they didn't anticipate to the logistics of getting where they needed to be at the right time. Regardless, let them raise their concerns and work as a team to prepare them for their next competitive experience. (*For larger teams or teams that compete in multiple events – Have your senior leaders and/or event captains lead these sessions by dividing them into groups of 6-10 students.*)

Third, give your students a chance to cleanup from the tournament if they haven't done so already. Debaters and extempers may have evidence or articles to refile, flash drives to clean up, flows to organize/clear out, scrap paper to toss, etc. Give them the time they need to sort through everything. This will not only help them get ready for the next tournament, but it will help them be more productive in the practices between tournaments.

Fourth, have students review their ballots. More importantly, help them focus their review of those ballots. The attached worksheet can be a useful tool. (*See "Debate Ballot Review" under "Debate – General."*) Students should look for common themes, threads, or statements from multiple rounds. (*They should also have their flows from the weekend next to them while reviewing ballots. In the process, they may discover their own ideas for improvement.*)

Speech/Interp Ballot Review

Name: _____   Event: _____

Tournament: _____   Date: _____

Rankings by Round: _____

Two things I can do to improve the delivery of my speech or performance of interp:
1.

2.

Two things I can do to improve the speech itself or cutting of the interp:
1.

2.

Two things I seem to be doing well, and should continue to do:
1.

2.

Debate Ballot Review

Name: _____   Partner: _____

Tournament: _____   Date: _____

Win-Loss Record: _____   Speaker Ranks/Points: _____

Two things I can do to improve my affirmative case/performance:
1.

2.

Two things I can do to improve my negative positions/performance:
1.

2.

Two things I seem to be doing well, and should continue to do:
1.

2.

Events (Speech & Interp)

Ice Breaker Interp

Early in the season, you should have two preliminary goals: 1) Build a safe community, in which students look out for one another, respect one another, and support one another. 2) Introduce students to the events in which they will compete. This exercise is a very simple community building activity that also gets them in the mindset of interpreting pieces of literature.

Description

Choose a favorite children's story/book. Familiarize yourself with the story, and then practice delivering the piece in the mirror to check your use of facial expressions, body language, and gestures. Utilize paralanguage (pitch, volume, pauses, rate of delivery, etc.) to bring the story to life. Your introduction should provide the name of the author and the title of the work, as well as indicate why you chose to present this particular story. In other words, what is the story, who wrote it, and why did you choose it? The intro should last approximately 30 seconds. The introduction & interpretation should take no longer than 5 minutes to perform. You should perform a cutting, if needed, to fall within the time limits of the assignment. You may recite the story from memory or present it to the class (or small group) as a storybook reading.

Due Dates

Students will perform their interpretations for the class (or small group) in two days.

(*Optional*) Grading Criteria

Interpretations are worth 50 points and will be graded on the following criteria:
1) Introduction - 10 points. Does the student clearly identify the author and title? Are relevant details (such as background information, historical references, etc.) explained? If needed, does the student provide an explanation of the characters or setting? Is the introduction brief?
2) Relevance - 10 points. Is the selection relevant? Does it make a social, historical, cultural, philosophical, or other important point?
3) Delivery - 30 points. Does the interper make the piece come alive? Are the characters easily identifiable? Does his/her emphasis, rate of delivery, and vocal quality/tone add to the interpretation? Is the student articulate and easy to understand? Does the student maintain balance between the text and eye contact with the audience?

Note: I identify the grading criteria as optional, because I am a firm believer in the importance of building a community. Activities such as this are far more important than any grade. While grading the assignment may motivate some students, it may also distract others from the real purpose behind the exercise.

Children's Story Evaluation

Performer	_____		Evaluator	_____
Title	_____		Date	_____

	Yes	Develop More	No	Not Applicable
Introduction				
Are the title and author clearly identified?				░░░
If needed, are background details provided?				
If needed, does the student provide an explanation of the characters or setting?				░░░
Is the intro clear, but brief?				
Relevance				
Is the selection relevant? (Does it make a personal, social, historical, cultural, philosophical, or other important point?)				░░░
Delivery				
Does the piece come alive?				░░░
Are the characters easily identifiable?				░░░
Does his/her emphasis, rate of delivery, and vocal quality add to the interpretation?				░░░
Is the student articulate and easy to understand?				░░░
If applicable, does the student maintain balance between the text and eye contact?				

Offer one constructive comment:

Offer one positive comment:

Impromptu Duo

Need a quick and easy exercise that gets students thinking on their feet while also developing characters? Task two students to put together an impromptu duo interpretation. Assign the students an impromptu duo topic and give them 10-20 minutes (depending on the skill level and confidence of the students) to put together a piece that they perform in front of the class or in small groups. Have audience members create ballots on which to provide comments and feedback to ensure they are using a critical ear when watching the performance.

Here are two methods of assigning topics to the pairs:

Scenario 1: I picked up this idea for assigning topics from a tournament in Florida. Choose three random items and require the performers to incorporate those items into the performance. For example, I might look around the room and name three random items that I see in the room: "clock, sock, and pencil" or "desk, water bottle, and football jersey."

Scenario 2: Keep two envelopes full of a) situations and b) descriptions of people. Have the pair select a situation and two descriptions. Then, have them fill in the details and perform it for the class. Some examples include:

Situations:	- Negotiating a movie to watch
	- Ordering takeout
	- Playing a board game
	- Buying a car
	- Woman in labor on the side of the highway
	- Entering an enchanted forest
People:	- Stay at home dad
	- Single mom with three kids
	- Engineer, nearing retirement
	- Pediatrician
	- Recently laid off factory worker
	- Starting quarterback for the Denver Broncos
	- Aging rock star

Selecting Events

If you let students choose the events in which they compete, create a handout that describes the various events. This helps them select the one(s) they would like to do. The following flow charts are examples you can use with your teams. Hand them out during the initial recruiting meeting in which your experienced students talk about and/or demonstrate some of the events.

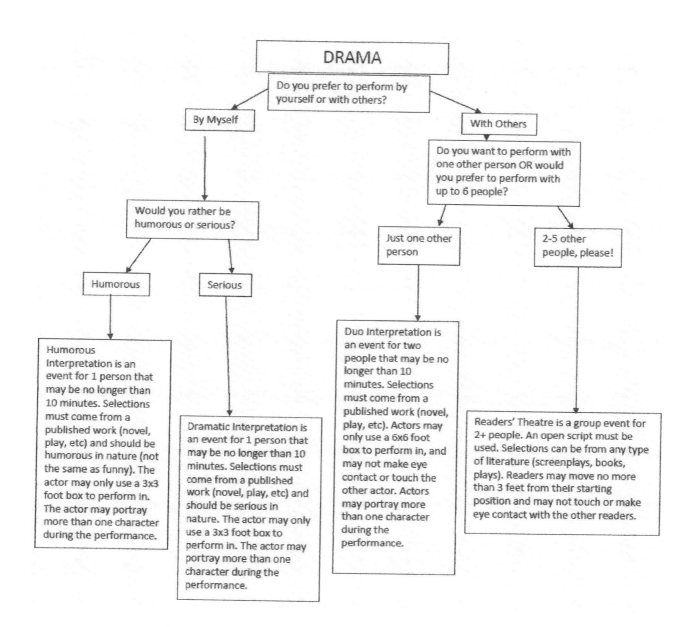

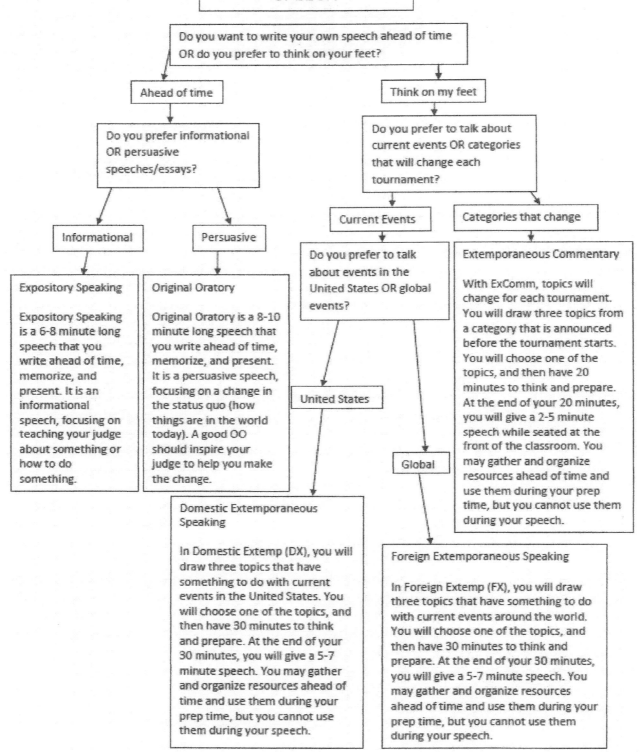

SPEECH

Do you want to write your own speech ahead of time OR do you prefer to think on your feet?

Ahead of time

Do you prefer informational OR persuasive speeches/essays?

Informational

Persuasive

Expository Speaking

Expository Speaking is a 6-8 minute long speech that you write ahead of time, memorize, and present. It is an informational speech, focusing on teaching your judge about something or how to do something.

Original Oratory

Original Oratory is a 8-10 minute long speech that you write ahead of time, memorize, and present. It is a persuasive speech, focusing on a change in the status quo (how things are in the world today). A good OO should inspire your judge to help you make the change.

Think on my feet

Do you prefer to talk about current events OR categories that will change each tournament?

Current Events

Categories that change

Do you prefer to talk about events in the United States OR global events?

United States

Global

Extemporaneous Commentary

With ExComm, topics will change for each tournament. You will draw three topics from a category that is announced before the tournament starts. You will choose one of the topics, and then have 20 minutes to think and prepare. At the end of your 20 minutes, you will give a 2-5 minute speech while seated at the front of the classroom. You may gather and organize resources ahead of time and use them during your prep time, but you cannot use them during your speech.

Domestic Extemporaneous Speaking

In Domestic Extemp (DX), you will draw three topics that have something to do with current events in the United States. You will choose one of the topics, and then have 30 minutes to think and prepare. At the end of your 30 minutes, you will give a 5-7 minute speech. You may gather and organize resources ahead of time and use them during your prep time, but you cannot use them during your speech.

Foreign Extemporaneous Speaking

In Foreign Extemp (FX), you will draw three topics that have something to do with current events around the world. You will choose one of the topics, and then have 30 minutes to think and prepare. At the end of your 30 minutes, you will give a 5-7 minute speech. You may gather and organize resources ahead of time and use them during your prep time, but you cannot use them during your speech.

Current Events Opener

Students of forensics should stay abreast of the news at all times. This is especially true for extempers, congressional debaters, and public forum contestants. A quick activity to keep everyone aware of what is going on in the world is to require students to keep an eye on the news whether it be through research assignments or simply reading *The Economist*, watching thirty minutes of *Headline News*, and so forth. Then, begin every class/practice by randomly selecting a student to deliver a 3- to 5-minute impromptu speech on a current event of his or her choosing. The student should accomplish two things in the speech. First, the student should describe the current event with enough details that anyone in the class could give their own summary of the issue. Second, the student should take an argumentative stance on some aspect of the current event. The 3- to 5-minute presentation also gives you the chance to perform any administrative tasks you have, such as taking roll.

Optional: Some coaches may offer an alternate activity for their students who compete in interpretation of literature. One alternative is to have them ready to analyze a specific aspect of their piece of literature. For example, the student may choose to look at relevant social/world events at the time the piece was written, type of literary elements utilized by the author, how the student's chosen work fits in with others written by the author, how the piece relates to current social/world events, and so forth. For the second portion of the task, the student should explain how he or she plans to utilize this information to better interpret the selection in competition.

Selecting a Piece

One of the most difficult processes in getting interpers up and going can be the selection of pieces for the students to use in competition. The following guidelines help students think critically about the pieces they are considering:

- There are numerous "for pay" options available for finding pieces such as those at 4N6 Fanatics and The Interp Store. These resources can be a great starting point for finding pieces, especially if you look at the pieces that have traditionally done well at state and national competitions. However, you need to be careful using these selections because other teams also access these documents, which means that students could end up doing the same piece as someone else at the tournament (or worse, in their room). Those selections are also the unique creation of another student or coach (cutting, introduction, etc.), so you should warn your students not to use them as is. They still need to go through the process outlined in *How to 'Cut' a Performance Piece.*

- Be wary of pop culture influence or the "movie effect." There are a lot of great scripts for movies that seem like they would be great selections for interpretation of literature. However, if the judge has seen that movie (possibly many, many times), it may be difficult for that judge to separate the movie performance from the student's performance. The judge may evaluate the student on whether he or she matched that director's interpretation and/or a specific actor's portrayal of a character. That is not to say movie scripts should always be avoided. However, make sure the student is doing an interpretation of the script—rather than an imitation of the movie—and be aware that some judges may evaluate the student positively or negatively based on comparisons to the movie they picture in their minds.

- Many of the most successful pieces come from literature the student finds on their own and is relevant to their life. Then, they cut the selection down into a workable 10-minute piece. They should spend their time in the "off-season" reading literature that interests them and noting if they think it will lend itself to a good cutting.

- Find a piece that the student enjoys and won't mind immersing oneself in for an entire year. The most successful pieces are those that are chosen early and performed at multiple tournaments, garnering as much feedback as possible, and revising throughout the year.

- When considering pieces for Humorous Interpretation, the main goal should not be to make the judge laugh. Similarly, for Dramatic Interpretation, the main goal should not be to make the judge cry. *The material should be light-hearted or serious, but focus on having the words and interpretation technique get the message across.*

- The material should not be too inappropriate—pushing the boundaries is fine, but most judges do not enjoy pieces that have a lot of foul language or inappropriate humor/topics. I always have the students imagine they are telling their piece to two different audiences: their peers *AND* an old-fashioned aunt/grandfather/family friend.

- Consider the student's strengths and weaknesses when choosing a piece. If developing characters through voice and posture are something the student is particularly gifted at doing, find a piece that utilizes many different characters to show off that skill. If the student has a talent for pantomiming actions, select a piece that gives him or her the opportunity to act out many interactions with the environment described in the literature. Ultimately, students should choose pieces of literature they feel comfortable with, because they will be spending a lot of time with it throughout the year.

How to "Cut" a Performance Piece

One of the best ways to ensure the student is passionate about the piece of literature that will be performed is to have him or her "cut" the selection from a larger piece of literature. This can seem overwhelming, particularly to new coaches and participants, but this guideline breaks it down into manageable parts. The following handout can help your students prepare for the upcoming year.

"Cutting" Your Interp

1. **Read, read, read**. The best way to find a piece that will hold your interest for an entire season is to read as much as you can from as many different genres and authors as you can. You can sign up for recommendations of new plays from various publishing companies, follow lists on Amazon and Barnes & Noble of new books that are coming out, as well as explore the classics. Some children's books and graphic novels lend themselves easily to Humorous Interpretation, so check out those sources, too.

2. **Determine what story to tell**. Once you have read many different books and have chosen the literature that you will cut your piece from, read the book again. Ask yourself why the story is meaningful to you. Why did you like it? Why did it resonate with your life? Most literature contains several story arcs, narratives, or messages. Identify the one that draws you into the story and makes you want to share it with others. This is where you start to interpret the literature. Think about the portions of the larger work that speak to that narrative.

3. **Cut the story**. Now it is time to cut the larger work down into something that can be performed during a 10-minute performance. Think about the portions of the larger work that speak to the narrative you identified in the previous step. There are two primary ways to cut the work. Different literature choices may lend themselves to one or the other, but it is also up to personal preference:

Path A: Cut the entire story
   Use the entire work from beginning to end, selecting bits and pieces from throughout that convey your interpretation of the literature.
   Pros: The story arc is already written, so you can follow it to make a cohesive piece. It is likely the whole story drew you in and made you choose this book, so it should have a similar effect on those who will watch your piece.
   Cons: This can be very difficult, especially with longer books. There is usually a lot of backstory that you will have to figure out how to share with your audience, without resorting to a 3-minute long introduction. Have someone who does not know the book read your cutting to ensure everything is clear.

Path B: Choose one or two major stories, sections, or chapters
   Select only the most relevant portions of the text as it relates to the message you identified in the previous step.
   Pros: This makes cutting easier, as the shorter stories contained in a work are usually relatively self-contained and are more easily adapted to the time constraints of the event. This approach works very well with collections of short stories or memoirs.
   Cons: There can be a lot of layered nuance in the book that relies on backstory that may not appear readily in the chosen section. Have someone who does not know the book read your cutting to ensure everything is clear.

4. **Map the story (of your interpretation)**. The steps after you choose your path are pretty much the same, though the culling of the story will likely be much easier with Path B – you may have to search a bit more to make sure that you have all the exposition necessary.

   a. Write out the arc of the whole story that you are trying to tell. Decide how many different characters you are going to utilize and what the best way to introduce all of them will be.

   b. You will not be able to tell the entire story, unless it is a short book, so think about what you can and can't leave out. Find a section of the book (probably 2-3 pages) that supports each of the major points in the arc, and copy those parts so you can mark them up as much as you would like:
      i. Exposition – who is involved and why they are there
      ii. Rising Action – creates tension
      iii. Climax – the big moment that will hopefully create the best response from your judge
      iv. Falling Action – deescalating the tension and bringing your piece to the resolution
      v. Resolution – wrapping up as much as you can

   c. Time yourself reading through what you have, and then figure out how much you need to cut to make the piece fit the time limits of the event. If you are under, go back to the book and find more material from the exposition and rising action to build the tension in your piece. If you are over, start looking for what is on the page that doesn't need to be there to tell the story.

   d. Continue to work the cutting until it tells one cohesive story with all five parts of the action. When you are done, have someone who doesn't know the book read your cutting to make sure they understand what is going on.

This may seem relatively straight forward, but it can take quite a while to get a good cutting of the piece. The goals of the cut piece should be three-fold.

- It should tell the whole story that you are trying to portray. This may not be the entire book, but it is what you have deemed the most important in the entire book.

- It should fit you well as a performer. Refer to the guidelines for selecting a piece. If you are very strong on voice development, use different characters to show off that talent. If you are strong with body presence and knowing how to move your body to illustrate ideas, seek something that has different body types or action sequences for you to portray.

- It should be your own cutting. There are many pre-made cuttings out there that anyone can pull off the Internet and perform as their own. You need to make sure your story fits your strengths, helps you work on your weaknesses, and conveys the whole story that you want to tell.

Peer Critiques

Students thrive on receiving critiques from their peers. Nothing seems to motivate them more than performing well for their friends, and they seem to take that feedback to heart. The idea of peer critique provides additional benefits for teams, as well. If your program is particularly large and/or involved in lots of different events, an emphasis on peer critiques allows the students to serve as co-coaches. This makes your time in class or at practice far more productive. In addition to providing benefits to the performers, the students who are observing gain additional benefits. They begin to see what judges see. This often translates to unique insights into their own performances, making them more effective communicators.

Before cutting students loose to critique one another, begin with an example for everyone. Have one of the experienced students perform his or her piece in front of the entire team, and ensure each student has a critique sheet in front of them. After the piece is done, have each student fill out the sheet on his or her own. Then, lead a class discussion to capture what they put on their evaluations. This allows students to see that even the novice students have valid feedback to offer (as it usually aligns with the feedback from the more experienced students).

Throughout the year, I assign certain groups to get critiqued during practice, whether it is by myself or by their peers. If they are on a peer critique day, they are responsible for finding three other students to comment on their performance. The performing group gathers all their critique sheets and reads through them, jotting down notes on their piece that they can use to improve. Then, they turn the sheets into me. This allows me to see what suggestions they are getting, which will help me to see if they are applying their critiques to improve their piece over the course of the year.

Forensics Critique Sheet

Name of Reviewer:

Name of Performer(s):

Name of Piece and Event:

Was this piece completely memorized? ____ Yes ____ No

Please identify at least one positive aspect of this performance.

Please write at least one piece of constructive criticism (things the performer should work on), and if you feel comfortable, a suggestion for how they could work on it.

Sample Forensics Critique Sheet

Name of Reviewer: *Amy Johnson*

Name of Performer(s): *Shawn Briscoe*

Name of Piece and Event: *A Child Called It, Dramatic Interpretation*

Was this piece completely memorized? __*X*__ Yes _____ No

Please identify at least one positive aspect of this performance.

I felt that Shawn really knew the material well, and was able to take a confusing story and make it clear for the judges to understand. His characters had distinct voices and characterizations, which made it easier to differentiate.

Please write at least one piece of constructive criticism (things the performer should work on), and if you feel comfortable, a suggestion for how they could work on it.

Although the voices for Shawn's characters were great, I feel that the physical differentiation between them could be better. I would suggest spending some time in front of a mirror to make sure that the differences are as visible as possible, as well as doing a video recording and then watching it with the script to jot down possible places for improved physical movement.

Making the Most of Rounds

As teachers, we all want to maximize the educational benefit of the activity. Debaters are inherently engaged throughout an entire round of competition as they actively listen to their opponents, think about potential responses, prepare speeches, and speak to the judge at the back of the room. Students who take part in speech and interpretation of literature are not so lucky. It is far easier for a student to give a 7- to 10-minute presentation then mentally check out until the next round. However, there is much to be gleaned from observing their competitors in any given room. As an active observer, they can learn important lessons about rhetorical competency that can translate to future competitive success. The following graphic organizer can be handed out to your students prior to an upcoming competition. Try giving them one copy for every round in which they will compete.

My Speech & Interp Log

Name: _____   Event: _____

Tournament: _____   Round: _____

List or describe each opponents' selection & your rank order of the competitors in the round:

Identify at least one thing that each competitor did that worked well:

Reflection after watching the other competitors. Lesson(s) learned/Things to work on/Things to incorporate into my speech/interp:

Debate –   General

Two Approaches to Coaching

Broadly speaking, there are two ways of approaching the education of your students as you prepare them for tournaments. Both are valid approaches. (*Very few coaches can effectively manage both approaches prior to the first few tournaments.*) Select the one that fits best with your background and expertise.

Debate skills focus: The first school of thought, and the one I employ, focuses on developing debate skills during practice sessions. Students use the skills they learn about how to build, analyze, and compare arguments within policy or value-based contexts as they explore the content of the specific resolution or debate topic. This approach uses practice time to start with rudimentary lessons on the basics of argumentation, moves into the structure of policy (or Lincoln Douglas or Public Forum or Congress) debate rounds, explores the foundations of policy (or Lincoln Douglas) debate argumentation, then finishes with advanced debate theory. Debaters use tournaments as a learning laboratory to develop those argumentation skills and explore the debate topic's content. You can find some recorded lectures of debate-related content on Shawn's website (**http://mydebateresource.com/for-debaters**) or through the National Speech & Debate Association.

Content knowledge focus: The second school of thought focuses on familiarizing the students with the content related to the specific debate topic. Coaches help students understand the material that will be discussed at tournaments. Then, students explore debate concepts while attending tournaments. (Still, I recommend coaches introduce two specific debate-related lessons prior to the first tournament: 1. Make sure you teach them the basic structure of a debate round in their specific format: speaker order, speech length, etc. 2. Familiarize them with what to expect at a tournament.) Several organizations provide lesson plans, activities, and primers on the debate topic. For example, The National Association of Urban Debate Leagues provides coaches with lessons plans, articles, and videos related to many of the core cases on the annual policy debate topic. In addition, the National Speech & Debate Association offers schools a Resource Package, which includes lessons plans, webinars, evidence packets, and more on its website. Simply login to the NSDA website. Once you login, select Resources, then Search/View All Resources. Finally, apply filters related to the format of debate you coach.

Introductory Debates

Looking for a quick activity to get students thinking, engaging, and debating early. Try this activity, which has two students debate in under 10 minutes.

1) Select two students (or solicit volunteers) and give them 3 possible topics... 2 fluffy topics & 1 serious (or vice versa).
2) The first student strikes one topic. Then, the second student selects one of the two remaining topics. The first student then chooses to represent the affirmative or negative side of the topic.
3) Give the students 10 minutes of prep time. (*Optional: Provide a graphic organizer for use during prep & speech time.*)
4) Time limits 1AC – 3 min. CX – 1 min. 1NC – 3 min. CX – 1 min. 1AR – 90 sec. 1NR – 90 sec.
5) Have the next pair of students prep during the debate, so you can hold another immediately after the first.

Additional Activity

Have new students sit next to varsity members/coaches. Have experienced members in the audience model flowing for the new students.

Fun Twist

Before the 1AC, poll the students to see whether they support the affirmative or negative side of the topic. Write the vote on the board. Immediately after the 1NR, conduct a new vote on the winner of the debate. (*Optional – Discuss the reasons for the final decision.*)

Example Fluffy Topics

The best teachers are those who upset us the most.

One's character is more important than one's reputation.

Social networking sites are good for society.

Imagination is more important than knowledge.

Extracurricular activities should be a grad requirement.

Money is more desirable than power.

Collaboration is preferable to competition.

St. Louis is a great place for youth.

Students should be allowed to have cell phones at school.

Example Serious Topics

Laws are more important than an individual's liberty.

All zoos should be outlawed.

The world would be safer if guns did not exist.

Labor unions are necessary to protect workers' rights.

Racial profiling is morally unjust.

Schools should require uniforms.

Violent video games should be banned.

Graduation exams are harmful.

Teachers should receive merit pay.

Corporal punishment should be used in schools.

Smoking should be banned.

Performance enhancing drugs, such as steroids, should be accepted in sports.

The media should show the full horror of war.

Contact sports should be banned in public schools

College athletes should get paid.

It should be a crime to spank children.

The U.S. should ban the death penalty.

Introductory Debates Graphic Organizer

Topic: _____

	1AC Case	1NC Response
	Exploring the Problem	
Current Situation or Attitude		
Problem or Goal		

	Exploring the Solution	
Benefit		

	1NC Case	1AR Response
Unintended Consequence		
Harmful Impact		

	1AR	1NR
Summary		

Extended Cross-Examination Drill

Need to work on ensuring your debaters are ready for the First Affirmative Constructive (1AC) at the next tournament? Want to give your students some practice asking and fielding cross-examination (CX) questions? Try this drill, which is primarily designed to ensure the 1AC knows the case inside and out. (*This drill can be used for the 1AC in policy/LD, the negative case in LD, the 1st Pro and 1st Con in PF, and authorship speeches in congress.*)

Select someone to read the 1AC while the rest of the class flows the case and jots down cross-examination questions. (*Ideally, there will be 5-10 students flowing and serving as questioners during CX. If you have a large team, divide the squad in half so the same exercise is taking place in two separate classrooms. While it is tempting to divide the team according to debate format — policy, Lincoln Douglas, public forum, congress — you might want to have at least two debaters from a different format sitting in as cross examiners. This division helps ensure your speakers are challenged in unexpected ways.*)

After the 1AC is over, have an extended cross-examination period (15-25 minutes in length). The coach should serve as a moderator to ensure the CX period isn't a free-for-all attack on the speaker. (*If necessary, when the 1AC gets stumped, let someone from the class answer the question. Again, the coach should serve as moderator.*)

The primary purpose of the drill is to familiarize the 1AC with the case, think about the types of questions that will come up at tournaments, and increase the speaker's confidence by living the experience before the next tournament.

Deepening the exercise: Select one person to be the First Negative Constructive (1NC). This person will not take part in cross-examination; rather, she will prep to deliver the 1NC. Then, conduct the same cross-examination exercise (for the 1NC) that you did for the 1AC.

Small Group Labs (Practice & Critiques)

One activity you can hold to help students practice outside of tournaments involves having them perform in small groups. Anyone, who is not actively practicing, serves the role of a judge or critic, filling out ballots (or providing commentary on notebook paper). This activity allows you to divide the class into small groups, all working independently while you focus on one group or float between groups.
- Break into small groups of 3-4 (by event)
- Within each group, each individual should perform his or her piece for the others

Speech & Interp
- The "audience members" critique each interp/speech as if they were a teacher/judge
    - The "judge" must offer at least one positive and one constructive comment per person
    - Critiques will be turned in at the end of class
    - Special timing for Extemp (3 people max per group)
        Prep time: 20 minutes
        Speech: 4-5 minutes

Debate
    - The "judge(s)" must give the debaters a judging paradigm prior to the first speech. *It is acceptable to provide a paradigm such as, "I'm a parent seeing my first debate round."*
    - Critiques will be turned in at the end of class
    - Special timing for Policy Debate (to fit a ~50 minute class period)
        Constructive speeches: 5 minutes
        CX: 1 minute
        Rebuttals: 3 minutes
        Prep Time: 3 minutes (per team)

Beyond the Cards

Debaters regularly become too reliant on their evidence files. One common misconception among young debaters is that a speaker must have a quotation to back up everything they say. Nothing could be farther from the truth. We want our students to think creatively and use their own ideas to deepen the debate. All too often, debaters use their cards as a crutch, replacing organic debate with pre-scripted quotations. Many judges complain that our students have difficulty communicating with their audience (since they appear to be reading from a script). In short, our debaters are too tied to the page. Ultimately, we want them analyzing the evidence, thinking critically, and engaging their opponents' ideas.

Exercise: Have practice debates in which the students are not allowed to access their files during their speeches. Have them prep with the files, but speak without the evidence packets in front of them. This will force them to think through the issues before they present them. It will also encourage them to make eye contact with the judge and communicate with him or her.

Deepening the Exercise: Send your varsity debaters to a tournament without any core files… no tubs… no laptops. Just pens, flow paper, and their best asset… themselves. *No, I'm not kidding. I've done this before*. Varsity debaters should know the affirmative case and major negative positions well enough that they can explain them. They should be capable of examining their opponent's files and cases using their knowledge of how arguments are constructed as well as by analyzing the quality of the evidence their opponents read. Many debaters get into the habit of relying on evidence packets and/or forgetting that there is a judge with whom they are tasked to communicate with during the debate. Even experienced judges who vote on the flow need to be drawn into the debate. They need to see/hear debaters thinking critically. This exercise uses a single tournament to force debaters to focus on those skills so that they can have a much more rewarding and successful experience over the long-term.

Cutting Cards

Cutting Cards Exercise: Throughout the season, debaters at all levels should be doing research to update the existing files. Once you have talked to them about how to conduct research (*I recommend scheduling time with the school librarian for that*), you want them turning those articles into useable cards. However, you do not necessarily want to turn them loose without a little guidance and practice on the process of cutting cards. After you have presented a lesson on what a good piece of evidence looks like, here is an exercise you can do to get them practice at actually cutting cards. Divide the class into pairs (*debate partnerships usually work well*).

Step 1: Ready Made Research. Hand out an untouched article, which you know contains potential cards. Have students work in pairs to bracket (or block) the relevant portions of text, which they might be able to use in debate rounds. After they bracket the article, have them write a 1-sentence summary or bullet point that describes the bracketed text. Finally, underline the relevant text within each bracket that makes the point.

Step 2: Share & Compare. Go around the room and have students share and compare the portions of text they found relevant. Also, have students share and compare why they think it is relevant...in other words, share the potential tag lines and relate the material to arguments they are making on the topic (affirmative case, disadvantages, etc.)

Step 3: Create Briefs. Transfer the cards to useable briefs. (*You can have them do this electronically or with scissors and tape.*) When they transfer the cards to briefs, encourage them to revise the tag from the original draft. They should also double check the power wording of the evidence. They may find that they need to underline more or less of the text. If using paper briefs, the new power wording should be done with a highlighter. If using digital briefs, they can highlight or change the boldface/underline. Either method is acceptable.

Adapting to Judges

As a communication-based event, it is critical that debaters learn to speak to their audience. This is the nature of persuasive speaking. If we fail to adapt to our audience, instead trying to force them to conform to our own understanding of what debate should look like, we lose the opportunity to learn how to translate the lessons debate has to offer about how to persuade people in other contexts. On the national circuit, many judges provide students with their judging philosophy or paradigm. However, these introductory comments are generally rather shallow, offering only a glimpse into the mind of that particular judge. On local circuits that recruit from volunteers and coaches, these pre-round insights into the judge are far less common. Nevertheless, students may routinely see the same volunteer judges and can utilize past interactions with them to tailor their communicative efforts to those judging perspectives the next time they see that volunteer at a tournament. The following handout can be distributed so that debaters can keep track of judges and adapt to them in the future. If oral critiques are given, students can fill these out while the judge is speaking to them after the round. If oral critiques are not given, they can be filled out the following week when students are reviewing ballots at practice.

Judging Philosophies

Judge: _____   Affiliation: _____

Tournament: _____   Round: _____

Physical Description of Judge (if name is not known):

Pre-Round Philosophy (if applicable):

Insightful Post-Round Critique or Ballot Comments:

How can I adapt to this judge in the future?

Making the Most of Elimination Rounds

As an academic activity situated within a competitive environment, it is not unusual for a select group of students to regularly dominate their peers at tournaments. Those who advance to elimination rounds have a distinct advantage over their peers. Not only did they already distinguish themselves in the preliminary phase of the competition, but they have the added benefit of getting additional debate rounds under their belt, they get themselves up in front of judges who may frequent tournaments, they (often) receive exceptionally useful feedback from the judges, and so forth. So, how do you ensure that your students minimize the risk of falling further behind their peers? Ensure that they watch elimination round debates. Sitting in the room isn't enough however. Observers need to attempt to engage themselves in the debate by thinking critically about what they are witnessing. As my former boss was fond of saying, "If you aren't flowing, you aren't watching." At a minimum, students should flow the debate.

You can extend on this by using one or both of the included handouts: A) Student Elimination Round Notes: This handout helps the student create a basic outline of the affirmative and negative arguments in the debate. It is, in essence, a modified flow and is especially helpful for novice debaters. To keep them in the habit of effectively tracking arguments made by the two teams, instruct students to use two colors of pens—such as blue for the affirmative and red for the negative—when filling out the handout. B) Elimination Round Review: This handout is designed to help students think not only about the round they just witnessed, but also to apply what they saw to themselves. Students should complete the handout while the judges are completing their own ballots prior to delivering the oral critique. Observers are encouraged to update the handout as they listen to the comments made by the members of the judging panel.

Student Elimination Round Notes (p. 1 – LD)

Round _____   Location/Date _____

Affirmative Debater	**Negative Debater**

Affirmative Case	**Negative Positions**

<table>
<tr><td>

Value

Major Neg. Response

</td><td>

Value

Major Aff. Response

</td></tr>
<tr><td>

Criteria

Major Neg. Response

</td><td>

Criteria

Major Aff. Response

</td></tr>
<tr><td>

Cont. 1

Major Neg. Response

</td><td>

Cont. 1

Major Aff. Response

</td></tr>
<tr><td>

Cont. 2

Major Neg. Response

</td><td>

Cont. 2

Major Aff. Response

</td></tr>
</table>

Student Elimination Round Notes (p. 1 – Policy)

Round _____   **Location/Date** _____

	Affirmative Team			**Negative Team**	
1A			**1N**		
2A			**2N**		

Affirmative Case	**Negative Positions**
Harms	**#1**
Major Neg. Response	*Major Aff. Response*
Inherency	**#2**
Major Neg. Response	*Major Aff. Response*
Solvency	**#3**
Major Neg. Response	*Major Aff. Response*
Advantages	**#4**
Major Neg. Response	*Major Aff. Response*

Student Elimination Round Notes (p. 1 – PF)

Round _____   **Location/Date** _____

Pro Team		Con Team	
1A		**1N**	
2A		**2N**	

Pro Case	Con Positions
Argument #1	**Argument #1**
Major Con Response	*Major Pro Response*
Argument #2	**Argument #2**
Major Con Response	*Major Pro Response*
Argument #3	**Argument #3**
Major Con Response	*Major Pro Response*
Pro Summary	**Con Summary**

Student Elimination Round Notes (p. 1 – Congress)

Round _____   **Location/Date** _____

Pro Speakers	**Con Speakers**
Cycle 1 - Main Argument	**Cycle 1 - Main Argument**
Neg. Response	*Aff. Response*
Cycle 2 - Main Argument	**Cycle 2 - Main Argument**
Neg. Response	*Aff. Response*
Cycle 3 - Main Argument	**Cycle 3 - Main Argument**
Neg. Response	*Aff. Response*
Cycle 4 - Main Argument	**Cycle 3 - Main Argument**
Neg. Response	*Aff. Response*
Cycle 5 - Main Argument	**Cycle 4 - Main Argument**
Neg. Response	*Aff. Response*

Student Elimination Round Notes (p. 2)

My Reason For Decision (RFD)

I vote for:

Reasons:

Judge's Decision

Name of Judge:

Who Judge Voted For:

Why Judge Voted:

Other Comments from the Judge:

Elimination Round Review (LD)

Name: _____   Tournament: _____

Date: _____   Round: _____

Affirmative Name	Rank	Points	Negative Name	Rank	Points

Describe the Aff. Value & Value-Criteria. (Be sure to include how they relate to the topic and why they are important.):

Describe the Neg. Value & Value-Criteria. (Be sure to include how they relate to the topic and why they are important.):

Describe the two best Neg. arguments/positions/applications of its case to the Aff.:
1.

2.

Describe the two best Aff. arguments/positions/applications of its case to the Neg.:
1.

2.

What was the best technique in the constructive speeches that you would like to work on?

What was the best technique in the rebuttals that you need to do more of?

Who was the best debater in the round? Why?

Elimination Round Review (Policy)

Name: _____   Tournament: _____

Date: _____   Round: _____

Affirmative Name	Rank	Points
1A		
2A		

Negative Name	Rank	Points
1N		
2N		

Describe the Affirmative plan, harms story, and advantages:

Describe the two best Negative arguments/positions:
1.

2.

What was the best affirmative response to each of those positions?
1.

2.

What was the best technique in the constructive speeches that you would like to work on?

What was the best technique in the rebuttals that you need to do more of?

Who was the best debater in the round? Why?

Elimination Round Review (PF)

Name: _____   Tournament: _____

Date: _____   Round: _____

Pro			
	Name	Rank	Points
1A			
2A			

Con			
	Name	Rank	Points
1N			
2N			

Describe the Pro team's initial arguments:

Describe the Con team's initial arguments:

What was the best Pro & Con response to each of those arguments?

1.   1.

2.   2.

What was the best technique in the constructive speeches that you would like to work on?

What was the best technique in the rebuttals that you need to do more of?

Who was the best debater in the round? Why?

Lincoln Douglas Debate

Lincoln Douglas Debate Lesson Planning Guide

Earlier in this work, I mentioned that there are two primary approaches to coaching: content (of the resolution) focused or debate skills focused. While both approaches are valid, I believe a debate skills focus is best for both Lincoln Douglas and Policy Debate. In short, those two formats of debate are unique in that they provide the pedagogical structures for understanding content, persuasion, and argumentation. For those who approach policy debate from the perspective of developing debate skills as a way to illuminate content, the following blueprint serves as a good roadmap for mapping out lessons. The needs of the season sometimes move these lessons up or down the timeline; however, the basic order ensures the concepts build on one another.

I also found it useful to have debaters of all skill levels sit in on these discussions. Frankly, a first, second, third, and fourth year debater will all get something unique out of these discussions. In addition, the varsity debaters keep me honest. They make sure that I do not skip over something vital, they point out changing trends in the debate community, and they challenge me with alternative perspectives.

In addition, I have my varsity debaters sit in on the discussions that pertain to other formats of debate. (For instance, my varsity Lincoln Douglas debaters attend all policy "lectures," and my varsity policy debaters attend all LD "lectures.") The "visiting" debaters often share unique insights as experienced outsiders. They also benefit by learning alternate perspectives that they can take back to their own format of debate.

Finally, you can find supporting materials for many of these lessons in other resources I have created. In some cases, I have uploaded lectures on my website (**http://mydebatersource.com/**) under the "For Debaters" tab. Many of these lessons have also been explored at length in my textbook (Briscoe, Shawn F., *Policy Debate: A Guide for High School and College Debaters*, Carbondale, IL: Southern Illinois University Press, 2017.) When applicable, I parenthetically reference the chapter of the text in which that material is covered.

Lesson -1: Welcome Back & Strategic Planning
The first meeting of the year should bring returning members and coaches together to discuss the team's goals for the year and establish a recruiting strategy.

Lesson 0: Informational Meeting
Meet with prospective students/team members. Highlight the team's personality, what makes the activity enjoyable, how the activity benefits students, etc.

Lesson 1: Intro to Debate
Introduce students to academic debate. This lesson often gets combined with "Lesson 0," since it can be the coach's take on the activity. Spend some time during this lesson examining the differences between the debate formats in which your team competes.

Lesson 2: Intro to Argument
Teach students the basics of argument construction. Explore what constitutes an argument, what one looks like, etc. This lesson can easily be combined with "Intro to Debate."

Lesson 3: The Lincoln Douglas Format
Introduce students to the foundations of Lincoln Douglas debate. Highlight the specifics of the format and introduce the stock issues of an LD case (aka – the value-criteria structure).

Lesson 4: Roles & Responsibilities
Walk students through an entire debate round. Explore the unique responsibilities of each speech. Suggest ways to prepare for those speeches.

Lesson 5: Cross-examination & Ethos
Explore two aspects of debate regularly overlooked or undervalued by debaters. Explain the importance of each. ("11. Establishing Credibility" and "12. Cross-Examination" of Briscoe, *Policy Debate*, 2017)

THE NEXT THREE LESSONS DO NOT FIT NEATLY INTO THE PROGRAMMING SCHEDULE. THEY ARE DRIVEN MORE BY THE TOURNAMENT SCHEDULE THAN THE LESSON PLAN PROGRAM.

Lesson A: Your First Tournament
This material should be presented during the final practice before the first tournament of the year. Students attending their first tournament do not have context for the logistics of a debate tournament. Walk them through the process of attending a tournament: etiquette, attire, behavior, reading pairings/postings, interaction with judges/competitors, expectations at awards, etc.

Lesson B: Competing Outside
This material should be presented 1-3 weeks before competing outside your team's usual circuit. Most teams compete in a relatively homogenous circuit for most of the season. The norms, conventions, argumentative strategies, and delivery styles vary between circuit & region. Before attending a tournament "outside the norm," take the time to prepare students for the expectations and differences of that "foreign" circuit.

Lesson C: Cutting Cards/Research
Introduce students to effective methods of research, as well as what a good piece of evidence looks like. (I rely on the librarian for the first part.) Show students how to cut cards physically (with paper, pen, and tape) or digitally (with Word, Verbatim, etc.)

Lesson 6: Flowing
Introduce students to the benefits of flowing and the best practices of taking notes in debate.
("13. Flowing" of Briscoe, *Policy Debate*, 2017)

Lesson 7: The Final Rebuttals
Discuss the final two speeches of the debate round (NR & 2AR). Explore the process and methods of delivering an effective summary speech.

Lesson 8: Controlling the Message
Discuss the ways in which a speaker uses organization, structure, and language to create a specific meaning in the mind of the audience. Use this time to highlight ways in which they can clear up a messy round or bring clarity to a debate.

Lesson 9: State of Nature & the Evolution of Government
At this point in the season, craft a lesson that is essentially "American Government 101." This lesson functions as a way of both framing the value-based analysis that came before and creating a bridge to future lessons that incorporate a more detailed look at philosophy.

Lesson 11: Philosophers and Their Big Ideas

This lesson is really a placeholder for a series of lessons on philosophy and values. There are two basic approaches. One approach is to organize the rest of the year around exploring various philosophies in a way that build upon one another. Alternatively, you may choose to craft philosophy lessons around the specific resolutions that are being debated throughout the year. In other words, when a new LD topic is released, determine which values are likely to be incorporated in the affirmative and negative cases on that resolution. Then, hold lessons on those values.

Lesson 12: Debating Without Evidence

Build a lesson that gets students thinking beyond quotations and cards. Help them to see that the best debaters win when they can pinpoint the flaws in arguments/evidence, rather than simply reading more evidence to the contrary. Explore logical fallacies. Get them thinking about how they can use other cards in their files to answer a never before seen argument.

Lesson 13: Judge Adaptation

Talk to students about the importance of adapting to one's audience. Discuss the various perspectives that judges hold. Discuss ways they can ensure they adapt to the critic that has been assigned to them.

Philosophy Week

Mid-way between the start of the school year and the novice competitors' first tournament, host a Philosophy Week to introduce first-year students to the philosophers and philosophies they will need to know and understand. At this point, you should have already taught students the basic structure of debate, reviewed the purpose of each speech, discussed the core elements of a Lincoln Douglas Case (value and value-criterion), and the purpose of philosophy in cases.

Procedure

Have a student coordinator or Lincoln Douglas debate team captain assign two or three philosophers (or major philosophies) to each varsity member on the team. Varsity members are charged with researching their assigned philosophers, creating a handout (*actual student samples provided on the following pages*), and planning a 3- to 5-minute presentation.

During "Philosophy Week," each varsity member presents his/her assigned philosopher. We recommend you begin with those philosophies that are most accessible and/or those that students may have been exposed to in other courses: Hobbes, Locke, Marx, Maslow, Rousseau, Thoreau, etc. The student coordinator/captain fills in any gaps left by the presenter and is always prepared to cover all philosophers if a varsity member is absent or does not complete the assignment.

For new teams and/or those without a large varsity presence, the philosophers can be divided among all debaters with one philosopher assigned to each student. In this situation, we recommend the coach cover the more complex philosophers/philosophies.

Katie Campbell
Ladue HS

Thomas Hobbes

1588-1672
English/Scottish
Major Work(s): *Leviathan*

Key Phrases to Remember
- Social Contract
- State of Nature

Philosophy:

State of Nature: Hobbes thought that the state of nature was a hypothetical condition of humanity before the state is founded. It is what a state is before there is a government or any other states' organization. In this state, Hobbes thought that people have the right to live, and they can do anything to help keep them alive. He wrote in *Leviathan* "during the time men live without a common power to keep them all in awe, they are in that condition which is called war; and such a war as is of every man against every man." Which means that in the state of nature since they have no one to kept them doing what they should do, like a government, it is essentially every man against everyone else. The state of nature was a nasty warish place.

Social Contract: Hobbes believed that the state of nature is followed by a social contract. The social contract was when people came together and gave up some of their rights in the hope that other would do the same. So they would agree that person A will give up his/her right to kill person B if person B agrees to not kill them. The system that came out of the social contract was anarchic and had no leadership, this was similar to the state of nature and could lead to war and fighting because there was no government.

Human Nature: Hobbes believed that humans are physical objects. He thought they were machines whose functions could be described in mechanical terms. For example, sensation is just a bunch of mechanical processes happening through the nervous system. Desires are just discomforts due to the mechanical processes. This idea, to him, produced the state of war.

Isaiah Berlin

1909-1997
British
Social and political philosopher
Major Work(s): *The Hedgehog and the Fox* (1953), *The Three Critics of Enlightenment, Russian Thinkers* (1978), *Historical Inevitability* (1954)

Key Phrases to Remember
- Value Pluralism
- Counter-Enlightenment
- Two Concepts of Liberty

Philosophy:

According to Berlin, philosophy is not just the unanswered questions, but also the questions where the way of finding the answer or the way to evaluate whether a suggested answer is reasonable is unknown. He also believed, like Kant, that while there is a difference between facts and the categories in which we try to understand the facts. However, he thought that the ideas through which we make sense of the world shape and are shaped by our experience, and as experience changes, so does the categories. Finally, Berlin believed that philosophy has a usefulness in society, and its goal was 'to assist men to understand themselves and thus operate in the open, and not wildly, in the dark.'

Value pluralism:
1) Several values may be equally correct and fundamental and there is no way to order values in terms of importance.
2) Values may also conflict with one another, which Berlin believes is "an intrinsic, irremovable element in human life."

For example, there is no way to tell whether being loyal to a friend and keeping a promise is better or more important than pursuing the truth, and the two can clash with one another.

Critics: Alan Brown suggests that Berlin doesn't take into consideration the fact that values can be compared by their benefits to society and thus are not incommensurable (impossible to measure or compare).

Counter-Enlightenment: Berlin referred to a movement that arose primarily in late 18th and early 19th century Germany against the rationalism, universalism and empiricism commonly associated with the Enlightenment as the Counter-Enlightenment in his 1973 essay "The Counter-Enlightenment." He said that pluralism was an unintended consequence of this revolt.

Two Concepts of Liberty: Berlin gave a speech in 1958 as his inaugural lecture as Chichele Professor of Social and Political Theory at Oxford called the "Two Concepts of Liberty." He argued that rather than our political terminology being understood as a single concept, each can have different uses and therefore multiple meanings. Berlin believed that these multiple and differing concepts show the plurality and incompatibility of human values and our need to separate them and switch between them rather than combining them into one.

The Hedgehog and the Fox: "The Hedgehog and the Fox" is one of Berlin's most popular essays. The title is a reference to a Greek saying that says "the fox knows many things, but the hedgehog knows one big thing". Berlin expands upon this idea by dividing thinkers and writers into two categories: hedgehogs, who view the world through the lens of a single defining idea (for example Nietzsche) and foxes who draw on a wide variety of experiences and for whom the world cannot be boiled down to a single idea (like Aristotle).

Lincoln Douglas Case Outline

Help your novice debaters by providing them with a suggested outline for their Lincoln Douglas cases. During their first year, I update this outline with the wording of the current LD topic and list some of the key terms I think they might need to define. Then, I print the outline so they can use it as a guide as they write their affirmative and negative cases.

LD Case Outline

Opening Quotation:

Because I agree with _____, I affirm/negate the resolution which states

Resolved: _____.

Framing:
Define key terms in the resolution.

Discuss the context of the resolution or discuss the affirmative/negative burdens it establishes.

Value and Criterion:

My value for this round will be _____, which is important because...

This value relates to the resolution because...

My criterion will be _____. This criterion achieves my value premise by...

Contention One (tagline):

Main Argument: Claim
Warrant (evidence, quotation, etc.)
Impact (analysis of the evidence and what it means in the round)
Relationship to the criteria & value

Main Argument: Claim
Warrant (evidence, quotation, etc.)
Impact (analysis of the evidence and what it means in the round)
Relationship to the criteria & value

Contention Two (tagline):

Main Argument: Claim
Warrant (evidence, quotation, etc.)
Impact (analysis of the evidence and what it means in the round)
Relationship to the criteria & value

Main Argument: Claim
Warrant (evidence, quotation, etc.)
Impact (analysis of the evidence and what it means in the round)
Relationship to the criteria & value

Flowing Lincoln Douglas Debate

Flowing (or taking notes in) Lincoln Douglas, Policy, and Public Forum uses a specialized notetaking method because arguments develop in a linear fashion over the course of the round. This means that every speaker discusses every argument—developing ideas further, responding to opponent's attacks, and so forth. Thus, each speech is flowed in a column, so that the next speech can be flowed in the adjacent column. In this way, debaters and judges can line up responses, see what was answered, what was extended into the final rebuttals, what arguments are new in rebuttals, etc.

Novice debaters typically have not developed a system of shorthand, perfected the art of writing small, nor to think in imaginary columns. Therefore, I instruct them to draw lines on a sheet of paper, label the columns with the appropriate speech, and flow with a landscape orientation. (I also have them do this on legal size paper.) Once they gain more experience, debaters usually transition to a portrait orientation so that they can add more depth on individual arguments. I have included a sample of what the novice flowsheet looks like. The first page represents the flow of the affirmative debater's case. The second page represents the flow of the negative debater's case.

AC	NC	1AR	NR	2AR

NC	1AR	NR	2AR

Policy Debate

Policy Debate Lesson Planning Guide

Earlier in this work, I mentioned that there are two primary approaches to coaching: content (of the resolution) focused or debate skills focused. While both approaches are valid, I believe a debate skills focus is best for both Lincoln Douglas and Policy Debate. In short, those two formats of debate are unique in that they provide the pedagogical structures for understanding content, persuasion, and argumentation. For those who approach policy debate from the perspective of developing debate skills as a way to illuminate content, the following blueprint serves as a good roadmap for mapping out lessons. The needs of the season sometimes move these lessons up or down the timeline; however, the basic order ensures the concepts build on one another.

I also found it useful to have debaters of all skill levels sit in on these discussions. Frankly, a first, second, third, and fourth year debater will all get something unique out of these discussions. In addition, the varsity debaters keep me honest. They make sure that I do not skip over something vital, they point out changing trends in the debate community, and they challenge me with alternative perspectives.

In addition, I have my varsity debaters sit in on the discussions that pertain to other formats of debate. (For instance, my varsity Lincoln Douglas debaters attend all policy "lectures," and my varsity policy debaters attend all LD "lectures.") The "visiting" debaters often share unique insights as experienced outsiders. They also benefit by learning alternate perspectives that they can take back to their own format of debate.

Finally, you can find supporting materials for many of these lessons in other resources I have created. In some cases, I have uploaded lectures on my website (**http://mydebatersource.com/**) under the "For Debaters" tab. Many of these lessons have also been explored at length in my textbook (Briscoe, Shawn F., *Policy Debate: A Guide for High School and College Debaters*, Carbondale, IL: Southern Illinois University Press, 2017.) When applicable, I parenthetically reference the chapter of the text in which that material is covered.

Lesson -1: Welcome Back & Strategic Planning
The first meeting of the year should bring returning members and coaches together to discuss the team's goals for the year and establish a recruiting strategy.

Lesson 0: Informational Meeting
Meet with prospective students/team members. Highlight the team's personality, what makes the activity enjoyable, how the activity benefits students, etc.

Lesson 1: Intro to Debate
Introduce students to academic debate. This lesson often gets combined with "Lesson 0," since it can be the coach's take on the activity. Spend some time during this lesson examining the differences between the debate formats in which your team competes.

Lesson 2: Intro to Argument
Teach students the basics of argument construction. Explore what constitutes an argument, what one looks like, etc. This lesson can easily be combined with "Intro to Debate."

Lesson 3: The Rules of the Game
Introduce students to the foundations of policy debate. Highlight the specifics of the format and introduce the stock issues.
("1. The Playing Field" and "2. Stock Issues" of Briscoe, *Policy Debate*, 2017)

Lesson 4: Disadvantages
Introduce the concept of disadvantages to students. Explore the key components of DAs: link, brink/uniqueness, and impact.
("6. Disadvantages" of Briscoe, *Policy Debate*, 2017)

Lesson 5: Speaker Roles & Responsibilities
Walk students through an entire debate round. Explore the unique responsibilities of each speech. Suggest ways to prepare for those speeches.
("3. Speaker Duties" of Briscoe, *Policy Debate*, 2017)

Lesson 6: Cross-examination & Ethos
Explore two aspects of debate regularly overlooked or undervalued by debaters. Explain the importance of each.
("11. Establishing Credibility" and "12. Cross-Examination" of Briscoe, *Policy Debate*, 2017)

THE NEXT FOUR LESSONS DO NOT FIT NEATLY INTO THE PROGRAMMING SCHEDULE. IDEALLY, THE NEXT TWO WOULD OCCUR AT THIS POINT. HOWEVER, THEY ARE DRIVEN MORE BY THE TOURNAMENT SCHEDULE THAN THE LESSON PLAN PROGRAM.

Lesson A: Building Your Tub
This material should be presented 2-3 weeks before the first tournament of the year. Assuming teams have not gone paperless, you should make time to teach them how to use their "tubs" effectively. Mountains of research are useless if they are not easily accessible in debate rounds. If your team has gone paperless, then take the time to familiarize them with your team's data storage/retrieval process and highlight functions in Verbatim (or whatever formatting system your team uses).

Lesson B: Your First Tournament
This material should be presented during the final practice before the first tournament of the year. Students attending their first tournament do not have context for the logistics of a debate tournament. Walk them through the process of attending a tournament: etiquette, attire, behavior, reading pairings/postings, interaction with judges/competitors, expectations at awards, etc.

Lesson C: Competing Outside
This material should be presented 1-3 weeks before competing outside your team's usual circuit. Most teams compete in a relatively homogenous circuit for most of the season. The norms, conventions, argumentative strategies, and delivery styles vary between circuit & region. Before attending a tournament "outside the norm," take the time to prepare students for the expectations and differences of that "foreign" circuit.

Lesson D: Cutting Cards/Research
Introduce students to effective methods of research, as well as what a good piece of evidence looks like. (I rely on the librarian for the first part.) Show students how to cut cards physically (with paper, pen, and tape) or digitally (with Word, Verbatim, etc.)

Lesson 7: Flowing
Introduce students to the benefits of flowing and the best practices of taking notes in debate.
("13. Flowing" of Briscoe, *Policy Debate*, 2017)

Lesson 8: Counterplans
Introduce the concept of counterplans in policy debate rounds. Discuss the four (traditional) stock issues of a counterplan.
("7. Counterplans" of Briscoe, *Policy Debate*, 2017)

Lesson 9: The Final Rebuttals
Discuss the final two speeches of the debate round (2NR & 2AR). Explore the process and methods of delivering an effective summary speech.

Lesson 10: Controlling the Message
Discuss the ways in which a speaker uses organization, structure, and language to create a specific meaning in the mind of the audience. Use this time to highlight ways in which they can clear up a messy round or bring clarity to a debate.

Lesson 11: State of Nature & the Evolution of Government
At this point in the season, craft a lesson that is essentially "American Government 101." This lesson functions as a way of both framing the policy analysis that came before and creating a bridge to future lessons that incorporate non-utilitarian perspectives of analysis.

Lesson 12: Beyond Utilitarianism
Introduce students to alternatives to the utilitarian consequentialist perspectives that define traditional policy debate.

Lesson 13: Kritiks
Introduce the concept of kritiks to students. Examine the key components: link, impact, alternative, and framework/role of the ballot.
("8. Critical Argumentation" of Briscoe, *Policy Debate*, 2017)

Lesson 14: Debating Without Evidence
Build a lesson that gets students thinking beyond quotations and cards. Help them to see that the best debaters win when they can pinpoint the flaws in arguments/evidence, rather than simply reading more evidence to the contrary. Explore logical fallacies. Get them thinking about how they can use other cards in their files to answer a never before seen argument.

Lesson 15: Judge Adaptation/Judging Paradigms
Talk to students about the importance of adapting to one's audience. Discuss the various perspectives that judges hold. Discuss ways they can ensure they adapt to the critic that has been assigned to them.
("4. Judging Paradigms" of Briscoe, *Policy Debate*, 2017)

Lesson 16: Performance Debate
Introduce students to performance-based approaches to debate. Help them to understand that performance is about delivery rather than a strategy. Discuss the origins of these approaches and ways to better engage performance debaters.
("9. Performance Debate" of Briscoe, *Policy Debate*, 2017)

Understanding the Affirmative Case

Make two copies of the graphic organizer (Understanding the Affirmative Case) for every student in the class/on the team.

1) Exploring a Problem-Solution through the stock issues of a policy debate case

Lead a class discussion on a topic of interest to the students. As a class, fill out the graphic organizer so that you create a compelling story for change. *Some examples of topics you might explore with the class: 1) Schools should require (or eliminate) school uniforms. 2) Public schools should eliminate contact sports. 3) Violent video games should be banned. 4) The legal voting age should be lowered to sixteen.* Regardless of the chosen topic, you should lead a discussion that identifies a problem, the cause of the problem, a specific solution/plan, and an explanation of how the proposal reduces the harm or gains an advantage. Once that is complete, then lead a class discussion that identifies potential responses to the case.

2) Analyze the affirmative case

Individually (or as debate partners or in groups of 4-5), students should fill out the graphic organizer using his/her/their affirmative case on this year's debate topic. Novices should be allowed to reference their First Affirmative Constructive (1AC) when completing the left side of the graphic organizer. They should also be allowed to reference the table of contents (or entire negative case file) that responds to the affirmative case when completing the right side of the graphic organizer. (*Students should not be limited by what is in the core files/research. Encourage them to think logically about additional responses they could make in a debate round.*)

3) (*Optional*) Extension activity

After students have had the chance to complete the graphic organizers for their affirmative case, have students share what they wrote with the entire class/team. This serves two functions. 1) It gets them up in front of people speaking. 2) It gives everyone a chance to write down additional thoughts/responses to the cases they may debate over the course of the year.

4) (*Optional*) Homework

Using the responses listed in the right column of the graphic organizer, have students prepare 1-2 answers they could make in the Second Affirmative Constructive (2AC) to each of the (potential negative team's) responses they came up with in class.

Understanding the Affirmative Case

The Affirmative Case

Possible Negative Attacks

Problem

The Affirmative Case	Possible Negative Attacks
1) What is the problem that you want to fix? (Harms)	What are three possible responses to the harms story? 1)
2) Why is this problem worth addressing? (Significance/Harms)	2) 3)
3) What is causing the problem? (Inherency)	What are two possible responses to the cause? 1) 2)

Solution

The Affirmative Case	Possible Negative Attacks
1) What is your proposal? (Topical Plan)	
2) How will the proposal fix the problem? (Solvency)	What are three possible responses to the solvency story? 1) 2) 3)

Stock Issues Identification

Early in the season, introduce students to the stock issues and the case areas/arguments on this year's topic. Once you have introduced students to the stock issues, you can use the attached worksheet to help students identify whether various taglines (or claims that will be supported with evidence) are affirmative/negative points and what stock issue those taglines point to in a debate round. The instructor fills in potential taglines in the first section. The students write the appropriate numbers in the second section.

Stock Issues Identification Worksheet

Determine which stock issue is addressed by each statement (or tagline). Then determine whether it supports the affirmative or negative side of the topic. Finally, place the line number that corresponds to the statement in the appropriate block of the worksheet.

#	Argument
1	The U.S. & China have taken action to address global climate change, but much work remains.
2	The U.S. federal government will substantially increase its engagement on decarbonization with the People's Republic of China.
3	Climate models show significantly less warming than the Affirmative's alarmist claims
4	Chinese government can't enforce CO_2 reductions
5	The U.S. cannot change domestic labor laws in China.
6	China is already addressing human rights issues on its own.
7	Climate change will be slow. No need to act drastically.
8	Plan draws China in and reduces tensions.
9	The South China Sea is a flashpoint. Conflict is likely.
10	Manmade global climate change could destabilize governments, create refugee crises, and cause sea levels to rise that in turn destroy ecosystems.

Is the plan necessary?

1) What is the problem? (Significance/Harms) *9, 10*	1) Possible responses to the problem. *3, 6, 7*
2) What is causing the problem? (Inherency) *1*	2) Possible responses to the cause. *6*

Does the plan produce a positive result?

1)What is the proposal? (Topical Plan) *2*	1) The plan is Non-topical. (Topicality)
2) Does the proposal make things better? (Solvency) *8*	2) The proposal fails. *4, 5*

Stock Issues Identification Worksheet

Determine which stock issue is addressed by each statement (or tagline). Then determine whether it supports the affirmative or negative side of the topic. Finally, place the line number that corresponds to the statement in the appropriate block of the worksheet.

#	Argument
1	
2	
3	
4	
5	
6	
7	
8	
9	
10	

Is the plan necessary?

1) What is the problem? (Significance/Harms)	1) Possible responses to the problem.
2) What is causing the problem? (Inherency)	2) Possible responses to the cause.

Does the plan produce a positive result?

1)What is the proposal? (Topical Plan)	1) The plan is Non-topical. (Topicality)
2) Does the plan make things better? (Solvency)	2) The proposal fails.

Understanding Disadvantages

Make two copies of the graphic organizer (Understanding a Disadvantage) for every student in the class/on the team.

1) Exploring the unintended consequences of an action through a structured disadvantage

Lead a class discussion on the possible unintended consequences of the action explored as a class earlier in the year (Understanding the Affirmative Case). As a class, brainstorm some of the potential unintended consequences (or disadvantages) that may result from the action you explored. You should narrow the list down to ones that you are certain can be developed into a disadvantage story with a link, internal link, brink or uniqueness, and impact. Then, let the class determine which one you will develop as a group. Finally, you should lead a discussion that identifies each element of the disadvantage. After you have filled in the graphic organizer's left side, star the elements that would likely be examined in the First Negative Constructive. Then, discuss some possible Second Affirmative Constructive answers to the disadvantage, which will go on the right side of the graphic organizer.

2) Analyze a disadvantage

Individually (or as debate partners or in groups of 4-5), students should fill out the graphic organizer using a disadvantage which applies to his/her/their affirmative case on this year's debate topic. Novices should be allowed to reference their evidence files when completing the graphic organizer. (*Students should not be limited by what is in the core files/research. Encourage them to think logically about additional responses they could make in a debate round.*)

3) (*Optional*) Extension activity

After students have had the chance to complete the graphic organizers for the disadvantage, have students share what they wrote with the entire class/team. This serves two functions. 1) It gets them up in front of people speaking. 2) It gives everyone a chance to write down additional thoughts/responses to the disadvantages they may encounter over the course of the year.

4) (*Optional*) Homework

Using the responses listed in the right column of the graphic organizer, have students write 1-2 answers they could make in the Negative Block (Second Negative Constructive/First Negative Rebuttal) to each of the (potential affirmative team's) responses they came up with in class.

Understanding a Disadvantage

The Disadvantage	**Possible Affirmative Responses**

Link Analysis

1) How does the argument apply to the affirmative? (Link)	What are two possible responses to the link story? 1) 2)
2) What other series of steps occur next? (Internal Links)	What are two responses to the internal links? 1) 2)

Uniqueness Analysis

Why is now the critical time to avoid catastrophe? (Brink)	What are two possible responses to the brink/ uniqueness story? 1)
and/or Why are we currently safe? (Uniqueness)	2)

Impact Analysis

What bad thing will happen as a result of the plan? (Impact)	What are two responses to the impact story? 1) 2)

Writing a Disadvantage

Once you have completed a lesson on disadvantages, you can use this activity to help students practice piecing together an actual disadvantage.

Preparation: Download a disadvantage file (on the current topic) from someplace like the National Debate Coaches' Association Open Evidence Project. At a minimum, you will want to print or create a digital file that contains the following cards:
- A link card
- An internal link card
- A brink card
- A uniqueness card
- An impact card
- At least two extension cards (link, internal link, brink, uniqueness, and/or impact)
- At least three cards from the "answer" file
- *Depending on the experience level of the students, I provide 10-20 cards total*
- *I ensure that, at least, three cards are incorrectly tagged, examples include:*
    - *A brink card with a tag that indicates it is a link*
    - *An overtagged impact card, such as a tag that says the DA ends in extinction, but the evidence only says conflict would be likely*
    - *A card from the answer file that is tagged in a way that makes it appear the evidence supports the DA rather than functions as an answer to it*

Activity: Divide the class into partnerships or small groups (3-5 students). Have them sort through the evidence and structure a disadvantage they could use in competition.

Step 1: Read the tags and evidence to ensure the cards are tagged correctly. Fix any errors.

Step 2: Label each card: Link, Internal Link, Brink, Uniqueness, Impact, Link Takeout, Non-unique, Impact Answer, etc.

Step 3: Select the 3-5 cards that best tell a compelling story and number them in the order students think will best tell the story in the First Negative Constructive.

Step 4: Share those disadvantages with the class. Discuss the differences between each group's "disadvantage shell" to include the strengths and weaknesses of each approach.

Step 5: Create useable files on paper or digitally. Your students now have a disadvantage they can take to the next tournament, complete with extension evidence and affirmative answers.

Crafting Counterplans

The handout on the next page has several uses.

1) Classroom Activity

Instructors can use the graphic organizer to conduct a classroom activity similar to those described earlier, "Understanding the Affirmative Case" and "Understanding a Disadvantage." Using either the affirmative case crafted in class or the students' affirmative cases on the current policy debate topic, work as a class (or individually) to draft a potential counterplan.

2) Competitive Template

Provide copies of the handout for students to take with them to tournaments. They can use the handout as a blueprint for writing a counterplan during debate rounds.

Traditionally, counterplans had to adhere to four stock issues. That is, the negative team had to fulfill four burdens when crafting a counterplan. 1) The counterplan had to be non-topical, so as to create a clear division between the affirmative and negative advocacies. 2) The counterplan had to be an opportunity cost of implementing the affirmative. In other words, if policymakers chose to implement one, they would lose the opportunity to implement the other. This promoted clash in the debate round. 3) The counterplan had to solve the affirmative team's harms story. This helped to keep the debate focused on the content of the resolution and the case presented by the affirmative. 4) The counterplan had to provide an additional net benefit to justify rejecting the affirmative proposal. This could be done by offering better solvency for the affirmative harms, gaining an additional advantage, or avoiding a disadvantage.

It is possible for a team to justify a counterplan without meeting all four of these burdens. However, the negative team must be prepared to explain to the judge why the counterplan does not need to be non-topical, solve the affirmative harm, or be a mutually exclusive policy option. If the counterplan crafted in the activity does not meet one of these burdens, you should require the student(s) to provide an explanation for why. Although this analysis might not be read during the First Negative Constructive, competitors should be prepared to offer it during later speeches.

Crafting a Counterplan

CP Text

Who?

(Identify the agent[s] that will carry out the action.)

What?

(Describe the action to be taken.)

1) The counterplan is non-topical.

(Provide, at least, one explanation for how the CP is Non-T.)

2) The counterplan is competitive.

(Provide, at least, one explanation of how the CP competes with the affirmative plan.)

3) The counterplan solves.

(Explain how the CP accesses solvency for the affirmative harms story.)

4) The counterplan is a net beneficial policy.

(Explain why the CP is the better policy option in the round.)

Understanding Kritiks

Teams can use this handout to analyze kritiks.

1) Prior to running a kritik, have students fill out the handout to ensure they understand the argument.

2) After encountering a kritik in competition, fill out the left side of the graphic organizer. In small groups, have a debater explain the kritik. Then, work as a group to develop potential responses to the argument.

The Kritik

Possible Responses

Link Analysis

1) What does the team say, do, assume, or use that triggers the harmful pattern of thought?	What are two possible responses to the link story? 1) 2)

Impact Analysis

2) How is this language, pattern of thought, or methodology harmful?	What are two possible responses to the impact? 1) 2)

Alternative Analysis

1) What is the alternative? 2) How does the Alt avoid the impacts and/or bring positive change?	What are two possible responses to the alternative? 1) 2)

Role of the Ballot

Is the role of the judge to: a) promote ethical education? b) vote for the worldview that produces the most desirable outcomes? Why?	Does the K function pre- or post-fiat? Does the Alt solvency story and RoB account for that? Explain.

Topicality Shell Template

Topicality – [*Word or Phrase in the Resolution*]

A. Interpretation

    1. Definition of [*Word or Phrase in the Resolution*]

    2. Violation [*Explanation of what the definition means in context of the resolution, as well as why the affirmative does not meet it.*]

B. Standards

    1. [*Identify a standard by which we should evaluate whether the interpretation is a good one. Examples include: predictability, field contextual, grammatical, limiting, etc.*]

    2. [*Include a second standard.*]

C. Voter

    1. [*Explain why the judge should vote on a topicality argument. The justification for voting on topicality usually comes back to the judge's jurisdiction to hear debate on the case, educational outcomes, or fairness in competition.*]

    2. [*Provide a second voter.*]

Flowing Policy Debate

Flowing (or taking notes in) Lincoln Douglas, Policy, and Public Forum uses a specialized notetaking method because arguments develop in a linear fashion over the course of the round. This means that every speaker discusses every argument—developing ideas further, responding to opponent's attacks, and so forth. Thus, each speech is flowed in a column, so that the next speech can be flowed in the adjacent column. In this way, debaters and judges can line up responses, see what was answered, what was extended into the final rebuttals, what arguments are new in rebuttals, etc.

Novice debaters typically have not developed a system of shorthand, perfected the art of writing small, nor to think in imaginary columns. Therefore, I instruct them to draw lines on a sheet of paper, label the columns with the appropriate speech, and flow with a landscape orientation. (I also have them do this on legal size paper.) Once they gain more experience, debaters usually transition to a portrait orientation so that they can add more depth on individual arguments. I have included a sample of what the novice flowsheet looks like. The first page represents the flow of the affirmative team's case. The second page represents the flow of negative off case positions that would be presented in the First Negative Constructive.

1AC	1NC	2AC	2NC/1NR	1AR	2NR	2AR

1NC	2AC	2NC/1NR	1AR	2NR	2AR

Public Forum

Public Forum Lesson Planning Guide

Earlier in this work, I mentioned that there are two primary approaches to coaching: content (of the resolution) focused or debate skills focused. While both approaches are valid, I believe the content focus is best for both public forum and congressional debate. In short, those two formats of debate are unique in that the topics change more frequently, are designed to cover a breadth of understanding as opposed to depth of understanding, and prioritize public persuasion over rigid argumentative analysis. I tend to approach coaching public forum students in ways that are similar to coaching extemporaneous speakers and orators. That said, I think they benefit greatly from sitting in on some of the Lincoln Douglas and policy-specific lessons. When reviewing the lesson planning guide for Public Forum, remember that I feel content-specific lessons usually take priority over these skills-based lessons.

Lesson -1: Welcome Back & Strategic Planning
The first meeting of the year should bring returning members and coaches together to discuss the team's goals for the year and establish a recruiting strategy.

Lesson 0: Informational Meeting
Meet with prospective students/team members. Highlight the team's personality, what makes the activity enjoyable, how the activity benefits students, etc.

Lesson 1: Intro to Debate
Introduce students to academic debate. This lesson often gets combined with "Lesson 0," since it can be the coach's take on the activity. Spend some time during this lesson examining the differences between the debate formats in which your team competes.

Lesson 2: Intro to Argument
Teach students the basics of argument construction. Explore what constitutes an argument, what one looks like, etc. This lesson can easily be combined with "Intro to Debate."

Lesson 3: The Rules of the Game
Introduce students to the specifics of the format, such as the coin flip, speaker order, and time limits. (*At this point, it would be beneficial to sit in on any structured lessons on things like Lincoln Douglas debate's value-based structures and policy debate's stock issues and disadvantages. This gets public forum contestants thinking about diverse ways to approach a controversial topic.*)

Lesson 4: Crossfire & Ethos
Explore two aspects of debate regularly overlooked or undervalued by debaters. Explain the importance of each.

THE NEXT THREE LESSONS DO NOT FIT NEATLY INTO THE PROGRAMMING SCHEDULE. THEY ARE DRIVEN MORE BY THE TOURNAMENT SCHEDULE THAN THE LESSON PLAN PROGRAM.

Lesson A: Your First Tournament

This material should be presented during the final practice before the first tournament of the year. Students attending their first tournament do not have context for the logistics of a debate tournament. Walk them through the process of attending a tournament: etiquette, attire, behavior, reading pairings/postings, interaction with judges/competitors, expectations at awards, etc.

Lesson B: Competing Outside

This material should be presented 1-3 weeks before competing outside your team's usual circuit. Most teams compete in a relatively homogenous circuit for most of the season. The norms, conventions, argumentative strategies, and delivery styles vary between circuit & region. Before attending a tournament "outside the norm," take the time to prepare students for the expectations and differences of that "foreign" circuit.

Lesson C: Cutting Cards/Research

Introduce students to effective methods of research, as well as what a good piece of evidence looks like. (I rely on the librarian for the first part.) Show students how to cut cards physically (with paper, pen, and tape) or digitally (with Word, Verbatim, etc.)

Lesson 5: Flowing

Introduce students to the benefits of flowing and the best practices of taking notes in debate.

Lesson 6: The Final Focus

Discuss the final two speeches of the debate round. Explore the process and methods of delivering an effective summary speech.

Lesson 7: Controlling the Message

Discuss the ways in which a speaker uses organization, structure, and language to create a specific meaning in the mind of the audience. Explore the techniques speakers use to persuasively frame the discussion on a controversial topic---This includes how they can frame the judge's perceptions and direct how their opponents respond to issues. Use this time to highlight ways in which they can clear up a messy round or bring clarity to a debate.

Lesson 8: Debating Without Evidence

Build a lesson that gets students thinking beyond quotations and cards. Help them to see that the best debaters win when they can pinpoint the flaws in arguments/evidence, rather than simply reading more evidence to the contrary. Explore logical fallacies. Get them thinking about how they can use other cards in their files to answer a never before seen argument.

Flowing Public Forum

Flowing (or taking notes in) Lincoln Douglas, Policy, and Public Forum uses a specialized notetaking method because arguments develop in a linear fashion over the course of the round. This means that every speaker discusses every argument—developing ideas further, responding to opponent's attacks, and so forth. Thus, each speech is flowed in a column, so that the next speech can be flowed in the adjacent column. In this way, debaters and judges can line up responses, see what was answered, what was extended into the final rebuttals, what arguments are new in rebuttals, etc.

Novice debaters typically have not developed a system of shorthand, perfected the art of writing small, nor to think in imaginary columns. Therefore, I instruct them to draw lines on a sheet of paper, label the columns with the appropriate speech, and flow with a landscape orientation. (I also have them do this on legal size paper.) Once they gain more experience, debaters usually transition to a portrait orientation so that they can add more depth on individual arguments. I have included a sample of what the novice flowsheet looks like. The first page represents the flow of the opening team's case. The second page represents the flow of closing team's case.

	1st Team
	2nd Team
	1st Team
	2nd Team
	1st Team
	2nd Team
	1st Team
	2nd Team

2nd Team	1st Team	2nd Team	1st Team	2nd Team	1st Team	2nd Team

Student Congress

Student Congress Lesson Planning Guide

Earlier in this work, I mentioned that there are two primary approaches to coaching: content (of the resolution) focused or debate skills focused. While both approaches are valid, I believe the content focus is best for both public forum and congressional debate. In short, those two formats of debate are unique in that the topics change more frequently, are designed to cover a breadth of understanding as opposed to depth of understanding, and prioritize public persuasion over rigid argumentative analysis. I tend to approach coaching public forum students in ways that are similar to coaching extemporaneous speakers and orators. That said, I think they benefit greatly from sitting in on some of the Lincoln Douglas and policy-specific lessons. When reviewing the lesson planning guide for Public Forum, remember that I feel content-specific lessons usually take priority over these skills-based lessons.

Lesson -1: Welcome Back & Strategic Planning
The first meeting of the year should bring returning members and coaches together to discuss the team's goals for the year and establish a recruiting strategy.

Lesson 0: Informational Meeting
Meet with prospective students/team members. Highlight the team's personality, what makes the activity enjoyable, how the activity benefits students, etc.

Lesson 1: Intro to Debate
Introduce students to academic debate. This lesson often gets combined with "Lesson 0," since it can be the coach's take on the activity. Spend some time during this lesson examining the differences between the debate formats in which your team competes.

Lesson 2: Intro to Argument
Teach students the basics of argument construction. Explore what constitutes an argument, what one looks like, etc. This lesson can easily be combined with "Intro to Debate."

Lesson 3: The Rules of the Game
Introduce students to the specifics of the format. This lesson should include speaker responsibilities, parliamentary procedure, and the difference between a bill and a resolution. (*At this point, it would be beneficial to sit in on any structured lessons on things like Lincoln Douglas debate's value-based structures and policy debate's stock issues and disadvantages. This gets congressional debaters thinking about diverse ways to approach a controversial topic.*)

Lesson 4: Cross-examination & Ethos
Explore two aspects of debate regularly overlooked or undervalued by debaters. Explain the importance of each.

THE NEXT THREE LESSONS DO NOT FIT NEATLY INTO THE PROGRAMMING SCHEDULE. THEY ARE DRIVEN MORE BY THE TOURNAMENT SCHEDULE THAN THE LESSON PLAN PROGRAM.

Lesson A: Your First Tournament

This material should be presented during the final practice before the first tournament of the year. Students attending their first tournament do not have context for the logistics of a debate tournament. Walk them through the process of attending a tournament: etiquette, attire, behavior, reading pairings/postings, interaction with judges/competitors, expectations at awards, etc.

Lesson B: Competing Outside

This material should be presented 1-3 weeks before competing outside your team's usual circuit. Most teams compete in a relatively homogenous circuit for most of the season. The norms, conventions, argumentative strategies, and delivery styles vary between circuit & region. Before attending a tournament "outside the norm," take the time to prepare students for the expectations and differences of that "foreign" circuit.

Lesson C: Cutting Cards/Research

Introduce students to effective methods of research, as well as what a good piece of evidence looks like. (I rely on the librarian for the first part.) Show students how to cut cards physically (with paper, pen, and tape) or digitally (with Word, Verbatim, etc.)

Lesson 5: Flowing

Introduce students to the benefits of flowing and the best practices of taking notes in debate.

Lesson 6: Whip Speeches

Discuss when to recognize that debate on a particular piece of legislation is winding down and effective ways of summarizing debate on that topic.

Lesson 7: Debating Without Evidence

Build a lesson that gets students thinking beyond quotations and cards. Help them to see that the best debaters win when they can pinpoint the flaws in arguments/evidence, rather than simply reading more evidence to the contrary. Explore logical fallacies. Get them thinking about how they can use other cards in their files to answer a never before seen argument.

Congressional Research Template

All formats of debate require students to engage in meaningful research. Teams should develop templates for that research in the form of briefs, which can be used by students before and during competition. The following (sample) template ensures that your team's research is both uniform and functional. This guide is especially helpful for teaching novices how to prepare research and allows them to contribute to the overall success of the program early in their first season. The template also allows coaches or student leaders to quickly review the evidence for acceptability, usefulness, and errors.

Aff/Neg: Name of Bill/Resolution (Font Size 14)

Quotes: (2-3 quotes minimum)

"Quote"
- Person quoted, what they're known for

ie:
"It's a lot more difficult because with euthanasia, the life wants to be taken. So you can't say, 'Poor fetus, nobody asked the fetus.' It's, 'Poor old guy, somebody asked him and he said, please do it."
 -Nigel Cameron, President of the Center for Policy on Emerging Technologies

Evidence: (8 card minimum with at least 3 per side, size 11 for bolded/underlined, size 8 for everything else)

1. _____

Source+Date

Evidence: cut and formatted

ie:

1. It's ethical

Tyson, Peter. **PBS NOVA**. "The Hippocratic Oath Today". **March 27, 2001.**

The Hippocratic Oath is one of the oldest binding documents in history. Written in antiquity, **its principles are held sacred by doctors to this day: treat the sick to the best of one's ability, preserve patient privacy, teach the secrets of medicine to the next generation,** and so on."The Oath of Hippocrates,"holds the American Medical Association's Code of Medical Ethics (1996 edition),"has remained in Western civilization as an expression of ideal conduct for the physician.". . .**Most especially must I tread with care in matters of life and death. If it is given me to save a life, all thanks. But it may also be within my power to take a life; this awesome responsibility must be faced with great humbleness and awareness of my own frailty."**

Flowing Congressional Debate

Flowing congressional debate poses some challenges because it is not as linear as most other formats practiced in the United States. That is, it is not as common for a line of argument to extend through every speech. Instead, most speakers accomplish two tasks. 1) Refute the main points of the previous speaker. 2) Add something new to the debate. Therefore, I find that flowing the debate in large squares (rather than the columns used in Lincoln Douglas, policy, and public forum) works much better for congressional debate. I built this flowsheet in Excel and print it on legal size paper with a portrait orientation. That allows me to have eight cycles on a single flowsheet. (*The sample in this book only contains six cycles because it is on 8.5" x 11" paper.*)

Congress Flow Sheet

1st Cycle Pro (1CP)	1CC response to 1CP	1st Cycle Con (1CC)	2CP response to 1CC
2nd Cycle Pro (2CP)	2CC response to 2CP	2nd Cycle Con (2CC)	3CP response to 2CC
3rd Cycle Pro (3CP)	3CC response to 3CP	3rd Cycle Con (3CC)	4CP response to 3CC
4th Cycle Pro (4CP)	4CC response to 4CP	4th Cycle Con (4CC)	5CP response to 4CC
5th Cycle Pro (5CP)	5CC response to 5CP	5th Cycle Con (5CC)	6CP response to 5CC
6th Cycle Pro (6CP)	6CC response to 6CP	6th Cycle Con (6CC)	

About the Authors

Molly K. Beck fell in love with speech and debate while student teaching at Parkway South High School. She firmly believes in using the activity to empower students and help them find their voices. Her coaching philosophy is rooted in each student having fun, learning, and experiencing growth. Molly teaches social studies and is the head coach of the speech and debate team at Ladue Horton Watkins High School in Saint Louis, Missouri. She has been the head coach of the program for six years. She coached the 2015 Policy Debate Missouri State Champions and in 2013 one of her students placed third in Impromptu Speaking at the National Speech & Debate Association (NSDA) National Championship Tournament.

She is the President of the Greater Saint Louis Speech Association; a member of the Eastern Missouri NSDA District Committee; the Saint Louis representative for the Speech, Debate, and Theatre Advisory Committee for the Missouri State High School Activities Association; and the Vice President-Elect of the Speech and Theatre Association of Missouri. She was the 2014 recipient of the Board of Governors Outstanding Young Teacher Award from the Speech and Theatre Association of Missouri. Molly attended Missouri State University and received a B.S. ed. in Speech and Theatre Education and a B.A. in Political Science.

Shawn F. Briscoe has spent more than a quarter century immersed in the world of academic speech and debate. He believes in the power of the activity and actively seeks to help others reap the benefits of it. After competing in policy debate and extemporaneous speaking for the U.S. Air Force Academy, he served as a commissioned officer in the Air Force. While serving, he volunteered with local speech and debate teams. Eventually, he transitioned to the world of education, coaching and teaching at Ft. Walton Beach High School (FL), South Anchorage High School (AK), and the University of Alaska Anchorage. He currently serves as the Program Director for the Saint Louis Urban Debate League. He has served in various leadership capacities in local and regional leagues, and he and his students have earned awards at local, regional, and national levels. Visit his website for additional resources: mydebateresource.com

Additional Books by Shawn F. Briscoe

Policy Debate: A Guide for High School and College Debaters, Carbondale, IL: Southern Illinois
        University Press, 2017.
Why Debate: Transformed by Academic Discourse, IL: My Debate Resources, 2016.

Selected Articles by Shawn F. Briscoe

"Forensics: A Socio-Emotional Learning Space," *Rostrum*, December 2008, p. 57-58.
"Forensics: Enhancing Civic Literacy and Democracy," *Principal Leadership*, May 2009, p. 44-49.
"Intellectual Combat: My Journey in Competitive Forensics," *Education Next*, Winter 2009, p. 88.

Amy J. Johnson's love for theatre began early in her life, but really developed when she was cast in her first play in 7th grade. As she continued through middle school and high school, she was given the chance to participate in a myriad of performances, both on stage and behind the scenes. She directed her first one act play as a junior in high school.

In college, Amy spent most of her time working behind the scenes, playing in pit orchestras and working on costumes and makeup. When she took her first job in Homer, Alaska, she learned about Drama, Debate, and Forensics (DDF) and was hired as the Assistant Theatre Coach. The next year, she was promoted to Head Coach, a capacity in which she has served for seven years. She has coached many students to State Championships and was voted the Alaska DDF Coach of the Year by her peers in 2012. She is the current President of the Alaska DDF Coaches Association. She believes the educational opportunities provided by Speech and Debate should be available to all interested students, and she focuses on the academic and team-building value that is intrinsic to this type of competition.

Praise

Policy Debate: A Guide for High School & College Debaters

2016 Finalist for Education
Foreword INDIES Book of the Year

"Policy Debate fulfills the need for a current, detailed textbook by preparing students for a variety of competitive settings."
Tara Tate, Glenbrooks South

"Students, and even coaches, often must attend summer camps at great expense or spend years working concertedly to gather the information clearly conveyed here."
Derek Buescher, University of Puget Sound

Why Debate: Transformed by Academic Discourse

★★★★★

Foreword **Clarion Reviews**

★★★★★

Readers' Favorite

RECOMMENDED
U.S. Review of Books

"Why Debate uses a perfect blend of academic argument and personal anecdote to prove the direct impacts that debating has on student achievement, civic engagement, and crucial skill development."
J. Scott Wunn, Executive Director, National Speech & Debate Association

"A great resource for students and coaches!"
National Speech & Debate Association

Made in the USA
Lexington, KY
26 February 2018